The ART of the FISHING FLY

The ART of the FISHING FLY

Foreword by PRESIDENT JIMMY CARTER

TONY LOLLI

With *photography by* BRUCE CURTIS

Preface by Glenn Pontier
Executive Director of the Catskill Fly Fishing Center & Museum

STERLING
New York

STERLING
New York

An Imprint of Sterling Publishing Co., Inc.
1166 Avenue of the Americas
New York, NY 10036

ISBN 978-1-4549-2902-4

Distributed in Canada by Sterling Publishing Co., Inc.,
c/o Canadian Manda Group, 664 Annette Street
Toronto, Ontario, M6S 2C8, Canada
Distributed in the United Kingdom by GMC Distribution Services
Castle Place, 166 High Street, Lewes, East Sussex, BN7 1XU, England
Distributed in Australia by NewSouth Books
45 Beach Street, Coogee, NSW 2034, Australia

For information about custom editions, special sales, and
premium and corporate purchases, please contact Sterling Special Sales
at 800-805-5489 or specialsales@sterlingpublishing.com.

Manufactured in Canada

2 4 6 8 10 9 7 5 3 1

sterlingpublishing.com

Interior design by Gavin Motnyk
Cover design by Igor Satanovsky
Picture credits can be found on page 226

A half-century has passed since I began fly fishing, so you might imagine how many fly fishers have influenced me. Unfortunately, many names are forgotten. However, one of my contemporaries, James Krul, and I go back forty years and we still fish together. Jim is one of those "been there, done that" of the fly fishing world. He owned a fly tying materials catalog company and served, for ten years, as the director of the Catskill Fly Fishing Center & Museum. Of late, he authored his own book on collecting antique fly fishing equipment. I learned a lot from Jim as we shared adult beverages and cheap cigars in numerous fly fishing camps in northern New England over the years. I suspect he's withholding more information until our next outing.

—TONY LOLLI

To Lorraine Gilligan, President Jimmy Carter, Sue Anne King, Michael Coe, and to all my other good friends who helped me with this project.

—BRUCE CURTIS

CONTENTS

PART ONE

EQUIPMENT AND HOW-TOS

PART TWO

THE FLIES

PART THREE

FLY FISHING SITES AROUND THE WORLD

FOREWORD

ROSALYNN AND I SHARE MANY MEMORIES OF FLY FISHING. We are fortunate to have fished across the United States and in many foreign countries. Regardless of the venue, we enjoy the camaraderie shared among fly fishers.

Although it's all fly fishing, brook trout in northern Georgia's Chattahoochee River require different enticements than do the huge rainbow trout of western Alaska's Copper River. The same flies used for taimen in Mongolia's Eg River won't fool the wild brown trout of Pennsylvania's Spruce Creek. Sea-run brown trout in Argentina prefer flies not appreciated by rainbow trout on Russia's Kamchatka Peninsula.

The comparisons could go on with differences noted for every type of fish. However, one commonality links these experiences: the fly. The device that defines fly fishing is also the common denominator. The blending of bits of feather, fur, or hair is a craft thousands of years old. Regardless of the materials used, or the fish species desired, it is the fly that engenders success.

I know, firsthand, what it takes to tie an effective fly, having tied my share. Rosalynn and I have also benefited from the generosity of well-known fly tyers around the world. Through my own fly tying, I've come to appreciate the skill demonstrated by fly tyers such as those featured in this book, *The Art of the Fishing Fly*. Theirs is a devotion to an ancient craft—a craft that will be passed from one generation to the next for as long as there will be fly fishers.

—JIMMY CARTER

2017

Opposite: President Jimmy Carter trout fishing on Turniptown Creek near Ellijay, Georgia, May 1988.

PREFACE

IMAGINE YOU ARE AT YOUR FAVORITE RESTAURANT. The server comes to your table and proceeds to tell you about the daily specials. You set aside the menu and listen intently, hoping that your favorite seasonal offering is on the list. Now imagine that you are a game fish, becoming hungrier by the moment as you swim in your favorite pool. You, too, are tired of the same old menu and want today's special. Suddenly insects from a hatch begin to rise and you strike at the fly of the day.

This is the way we sometimes introduce fly fishing to individuals who know nothing about the sport—a group that includes most people who live in the United States.

Once you understand why fly tyers are creating artificial replicas of natural insects, then the door opens and it is possible to understand some of the fascination and complexity of this remarkable craft.

This amazing book is exactly the right introduction for those new to fly fishing and fly tying, and the perfect tome for those who already love and partake of the sport. Many visitors to the Catskill Fly Fishing Center & Museum (CFFCM) know a thing or two about fly fishing—or they soon learn.

The sport originated in the Catskills because of the abundance of water running through the numerous mountain streams. The weather and geology of these mountains combine in a unique way to provide a wealth of water unlike any other place on earth. New York City draws off 800 million gallons every day through vast tunnels over 100 miles long. At the same time, Philadelphia relies on the heavy flow of freshwater streaming down the Delaware River to hold back the ocean salt pushing up Delaware Bay.

For the past thirty-six years, the museum has been telling this story of earth and water and insect and fish, and their intersection with humanity. Folks who are fly

fishers know all about "matching the hatch" and finding just the right dry fly to catch a trout. And they are fascinated by the items to be seen in the museum. CFFCM is the recipient of the largest private and commercial collections—of rods, reels, tackle, clothing, flies, line, and other fishing materials—in the world. These artifacts are archived in a permanent collection and displayed in changing museum exhibits.

Exhibits feature names like Elsie and Harry Darbee, Winnie and Walt Dette, Poul Jorgensen, Lee Wulff, and Art Flick—as well as a Hall of Fame recognizing over one hundred individuals who have made significant contributions to the world of fly fishing. Exhibits include historic monuments to fly fishing, the development of rods and reels, and numerous examples of fishing flies. At any given moment there are also new exhibitions of fishers, artists, writers, fly tyers, rodmakers, and environmentalists.

Walk into the museum with someone who is a fly fisher, and he or she is in heaven.

But those who don't know the sport are often mystified by this culture of fly fishing, where so much time and effort is spent to catch a fish that is then released into the water. For these newcomers, the museum is like an antique store with nothing for sale. Most of the names are unfamiliar, many of the fishing rods are made from bamboo, and then there are those little fishing flies.

What are those bug-like "things" with hooks on them? Who has made these beautiful, colorful miniature insects? Why are there so many different kinds of flies?

Welcome to *The Art of the Fishing Fly*, which tells this story through essays, descriptions, and enlarged photographs of the four major divisions of fly patterns. Like needlepoint, scrimshaw, quilt-making, and other traditional American crafts, the art of tying flies has a unique integrity and beauty found nowhere else. While it is easy to learn the basics, mastering this art requires a skill and perseverance found only by the truly dedicated.

Opposite: Sign welcoming visitors to the Catskill Fly Fishing Center & Museum in Livingston Manor, New York.
Above: A Poul Jorgensen exhibit at the Catskill Fly Fishing Center & Museum.

The museum has known a lot about fishing flies since its inception in 1981, after Elsie Darbee brought up the idea of preserving and sharing the trout fishing tradition and spirit of the fly fishing community. The Darbee kitchen in Roscoe, New York, was the place where many fly fishers gathered to exchange stories and advice about their chosen sport while they tied a few of their favorite flies.

Recently the CFFCM became the recipient of the Masters Fly Collection, tied by the world's preeminent fly tyers, past and present. This major new collection of flies is a three-decade-plus project curated by Tom Zacoi of Venetia, Pennsylvania. It includes over two thousand flies in nine museum-quality fly cases. Three hold 48 vials of preserved entomological specimens (representing the major hatches throughout North America) with flies tied for each life cycle stage of the insect's development. Three more boxes house realistic salmon flies, saltwater and bass bugs, and caddisflies.

The collection was tied by 575 people, including many in this book. They represent thirty-two countries, including: Argentina, Australia, Austria, Belgium, Bulgaria, Canada, Chile, Denmark, Fiji, Finland, France, Germany, Greece, Holland, Iceland, Ireland, Italy, Japan, Lithuania, New Zealand, Norway, Pakistan, Poland, Scotland, Slovenia, Spain, Sweden, Ukraine, the

Fly and leader boxes on display at the Museum.

United Kingdom, the United States, and Wales. The collection is housed in the museum's archive, with major exhibits scheduled in 2018 and 2020.

The mission of the Catskill Fly Fishing Center & Museum is to preserve the past, protect the present, and promote the future of fly fishing. This interaction of history and the future is played out every day on its grounds.

This is the place where people come to share the collective story of fly fishing after they have been hooked on a sport that places artistry and nature and healing at the forefront of its values. There is a therapeutic value to standing in a clean mountain stream, casting one's line with a hand-tied fly on the end, wrestling with a beautiful game fish . . . and then releasing it unharmed back to nature.

The culture of fly fishing lives here in this museum. An appreciation of the lore and art that is the fishing fly can be found in this book.

—GLENN PONTIER

2017

A view of flags, flies, and other memorabilia from around the world at the Museum.

INTRODUCTION

"If fishing is a religion, fly fishing is high church."
—Tom Brokaw, 1991

Some fly fishers dance with rivers. They belong to a clan that is generations old. Some say it began with the ancient Greeks; others say it was the Babylonians. Regardless, the fishing fly is their amulet—a touchstone to the ancient ones. Throughout history, the fishing fly has connected each member to its traditions, allowing them to become a contributor in spirit. Although the rod and reel remain constant, the fly has a multitude of variations, each with singular intent: to provide the passageway to active participation.

The fly fisher's dance may take place on diminutive, misty rills inhabited by brightly colored brook trout—the jeweled, lightweight trout. It might take place on larger streams where cagey, rapacious brown and rainbow trout challenge the tribe's skills. Or the dance might be held on big-shouldered rivers that dare them to risk safety for the prize of hidden Atlantic salmon. Whatever the venue, the fly is the key *and* the path.

The fly takes many forms. Some retain ancient elements, while others have evolved into modern versions. Regardless, the intended function is pure: to enable fly fishers to become active participants in the ancient dance.

This book provides insight into, and appreciation of, the lore and art that is the fishing fly.

Opposite: Fly fishing on the Battenkill in Arlington, Vermont.

OVERVIEW

The allure of fly fishing has evolved over thousands of years, from the necessity to feed one's family to the desire to feed one's soul. At the center of this succession is the fishing fly. It is an icon, and it represents more than membership in the fly fishing tribe; it symbolizes active participation in this segment of outdoor lifestyle.

More than 3.8 million American fly fishers carry the torch for the millions who came, and went, before them. Each era had its own fly patterns. Some are long forgotten, while others continue to prove their effectiveness. Even today, some look upon fly tyers as alchemists, conjuring up lifelike organisms from steel, feathers, and fur. Those fishers willing to take up the fly tying craft discover that there is more art than science involved. Materials and techniques continue to evolve, and this keeps the interest of fly tyers old and new.

More has likely been written about fly fishing than any other sport. No title, however, has taken a closer look at the emblem of this activity than this book. It is, then, the intent of this book to present the fishing fly for the art form it is. The delicate manipulations of materials result in objects of art designed not only to fool fish but also to please the eye of those who fish. Those who do not fish have even come to appreciate this art, and so some patterns have found their ways into shadowboxes, never to float upon water.

Some of the tools and materials needed for creating flies.

The Art of the Fishing Fly will give pleasure to tyers and non-tyers alike by presenting enlarged views of fly patterns. Every turn of fur, every proportion of construction, every color of feather will be clearly in focus. The presentation will amaze even those who have never felt the pulse-quickening electricity that comes with a fish's strike.

The four major divisions of fly patterns will be presented in this book. Atlantic salmon flies, the most colorful of all, have a 250-year history. They first appeared in the United Kingdom when the British Empire stretched around the world and made materials available to tyers from every corner of the globe.

Trout flies are the most commonly tied patterns because the majority of fly tyers fish for trout. Some patterns are so impressive that one waits for them to fly away. As imitations of natural insects they are unimaginably delicate, as demonstrated by the enlarged images herein; one marvels at the skill required to create such ephemeral art.

Trout flies in a fly box.

Saltwater flies are the workhorses of fly fishing patterns, designed to capture fish in the hundreds, if not thousands, of pounds. Tuna, tarpon, sailfish, and even giant marlin are taken on flies of incredible colors. Modern synthetic materials, in colors not found in the rainbow, are breathtaking when viewed in all their glorious hues.

Warm-water patterns are the newest to evolve, having originated only about fifty years ago. Bass, pike, and muskellunge take these patterns designed to represent baitfish, frogs, mice, and leeches among others. Unusual color combinations and natural materials such as deer hair are commonly used but seldom seen up close. The ingenuity of these patterns is astounding.

The presentation of all four divisions of this intricate art form will delight the reader, whether or not they are entranced by the seductive voices of wild places.

THE ZEN OF FLY FISHING

As noted earlier, more has been written about fly fishing than probably any other sport. What accounts for this abundance? Perhaps it is because fly fishing has been described as the contemplative sport. Perhaps this meditative effect goes deeper than our consciousness and influences us even when we are not engaged in the act of fly fishing.

Zen is characterized as a complete state of focus that incorporates a total togetherness of body and mind. Those who are lifelong fly fishers will tell you fly fishing is not a sport—it is a way of life. This is not hyperbole. It is always in the back of our minds, if not at the forefront. Even in winter months that do not lend themselves to the activity itself, fly fishers spend their time acquiring equipment and tying flies.

Flies have a special significance because they are touchstones that connect us to the fly fishing life, past, present, and future.

Were it not for fly fishing, there would be no need for fishing flies. They exist in a partnership nearly as old as civilization. Like many other ancient inventions, such as the bow and arrow or spear, fly fishing appears to have been discovered independently in several places and in different epochs.

The earliest written description of fly fishing is attributed to the Roman author Claudius Aelianus (c. 175–c. 235 CE). In c. 200 CE, Aelianus described the Macedonian way of fly fishing in his work *Varia Historia* (*Various History*):

> *I have heard of a Macedonian way of catching fish, and it is this: between Berœa and Thessalonica runs a river called the Astrœus, and in it there are fish with speck-led skins; what the natives of the country call them you had better ask the Macedonians. These fish feed on a fly peculiar to the country, which hovers on the river. . . .*
>
> *They fasten red (crimson red) wool round a hook, and fix on to the wool two feathers which grow under a cock's wattles, and which in color are like wax. Their rod is six feet long, and their line is the same length. Then they throw their snare, and the fish, attracted and mad-dened by the color, comes straight at it, thinking from the pretty sight to get a dainty mouthful; when, however, it opens its jaws, it is caught by the hook and enjoys a bitter repast, a captive.*

What astonishes are the similarities between Aelian's account and today's practice of tying flies of particular colors in order to imitate the appearance of an aquatic insect. The fly fisher, thus, becomes a participant in the natural order—a reflection of the Zen of fly fishing.

Some believe the centuries-old Japanese method of *tenkara* fly fishing was used as a means of "enlightening" samurai warriors when they were not engaged in warfare. Apparently, this was an important consideration in the twelfth century if the nobleperson was to maintain control of the warrior class during times of peace. This Japanese fishing technique blends the traditions of contemplation and personal challenge and is, perhaps, the earliest

Two people fish at a weir near Mount Fuji in this nineteenth-century print by acclaimed Japanese printmaker Hokusai.

notion of the Zen of fly fishing: a connection between angler and nature. Support for the assertion that fly fishing developed independently in different times and places comes from widespread twelfth-century Asian woodcarvings illustrating a man with rod and line arguably identical to what Claudius Aelianus wrote about.

Even older evidence can be seen in depictions found in Egyptian tombs at the Beni Hasan burial site, from around the twentieth century BCE. Once again, a person is seen holding a rod with a line of equal length and a fish on the end. It's interesting to note that some think fishing for recreation is a recent development; however, hunting and fishing were seen as both a sport and a source of food

Woodcut of a man angling with a simple rod from an 1880 edition of *A Treatyse of Fysshynge wyth an Angle* (1496).

by the ancient Egyptians. Other, more efficient methods such as nets and traps existed at the same time as this ancient angling. Were food the only endgame of fishing, traps and nets would outproduce angling. Thus, angling was an activity practiced for recreation.

The British tradition of fly fishing comes to mind when speaking of more recent forms. It is the image of a fisher gracefully casting a line that appears to hover of its own accord which provides the archetypical image of fly fishing. Even the British tradition is centuries old though, going back at least to *A Treatyse of Fysshynge wyth an Angle* (1496); an illustration from that book is shown here at left.

By the nineteenth century, dressings for flies were described and a standardization of sorts was established. The use of reels to hold fly lines also came about around this time. No longer would fishers be limited to a line tied to the tip of a rod. With the advent of reels came the ability to cast or throw a line. The fly went along for the ride and could reach distances not allowed by a line tethered to the rod tip.

With the spread of railroads, travel to far-off British and Scottish Atlantic salmon waters became possible, and the sport of salmon angling was available to anyone who could pay the freight. This time frame, the height of the British Empire, also resulted in the availability of colorful and unique fly tying materials from the colonies. "Full dressed" salmon flies, some of which can be viewed in this book, require tyers to faithfully adhere to established standards. Many Atlantic salmon flies incorporate as many as thirty different materials, tied on in a specific order using a predetermined technique. A small cadre of salmon tyers preserves these iconic patterns and passes their knowledge on to new tyers. In this way, they keep alive the tradition and their connections to an earlier time and place.

Contemporary fly fishers often speak of the sense of becoming part of the natural environment while fly fishing. For them, it is the total experience of participation that matters most. Many report that the process of discovering which insects are hatching, selecting an appropriate imitation, determining where and how the cast should be delivered, and sending the fly on a downstream drift that replicates the float of the natural insect all add to the moment. A couple of examples are in order.

The organization Casting for Recovery® is on a mission to "enhance the quality of life of women with breast cancer through a unique retreat program that combines breast cancer education and peer support with the therapeutic sport of fly fishing. The program offers opportunities for women to find inspiration, discover renewed energy for life, and experience healing connections with other women and nature." The repetitive motion of fly casting was identified as restorative for traumatized muscles, but participants quickly recognize a second benefit. They will tell you the act of being in a flowing river and focusing entirely on the tasks at hand create a healing experience. For a short time they are far from the worries and health threats they face in their everyday lives. They describe it as natural, healthy experience that is calming and makes them better prepared to deal with their cancer. This, then, is the Zen of their fly fishing experience, and it would not be possible but for the involvement of the fishing fly.

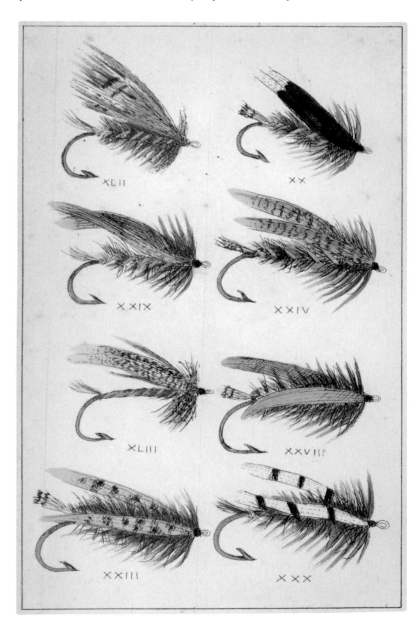

A color plate of salmon flies from *Rod-Fishing in Clear Waters by Fly, Minnow, and Worm*, by Henry Wade, 1860.

Project Healing Waters Fly Fishing, an international organization, is "dedicated to the physical and emotional rehabilitation of disabled active military service personnel and disabled veterans through fly fishing and associated activities including education and outings." Activities for members occur on a monthly basis, and, as might be imagined, the range of disabilities, both physical and emotional, varies widely. In spite of this great variability, participants are unanimous: being actively involved in the environs and activities of fly fishing is therapeutic and healing. Camaraderie plays an important role, because participants share the stories of their disabling experiences and know that others have gone through similar trials. Although volunteers may not have those experiences in common with the participants, they can all share the Zen of fly fishing.

When all is said and done, perhaps a quotation by Henry David Thoreau might best explain the Zen of fly fishing: "Many men go fishing all of their lives without knowing that it is not fish they are after."

PART ONE

EQUIPMENT AND HOW-TOS

*"There is certainly something in angling . . . that tends to produce
a gentleness of spirit and a pure serenity of mind."*

—Washington Irving, "The Angler," 1820

EQUIPMENT

Fly fishing equipment has changed over the centuries and often reflects the available technology of the respective time periods. Early on, fishers made their own rods, reels, lines, and flies. Specialists began offering these items for sale, and mass-production techniques following the industrial revolution kept prices low enough to meet the growing demand that accompanied more free time for workers. Following World War II, new materials began finding their way into fly fishing tackle, especially rods and reels. Some embraced the changes, while others lamented the lost art of handmade tackle. These two opinions remain diverged and to this day separate those who accept modern materials from those who prefer the offerings by individuals who make rods from split bamboo and handcraft fly reels.

Opposite: Bass rod with fancy cork grip and balsa wood bass flies.
Right: Fishing on the Battenkill.

FLY RODS

Some historians cite an illustration of an angler from the ancient Greek city of Thebes, c. 1400 BCE, as the earliest record of fly fishing. The angler is shown using a 6-foot (2-m) branch with a 6-foot horsehair line tied to the rod tip and a fly made from wool and a feather from the neck of a rooster. Rods at that time were collected near the river and were disposable.

The next major fly rod advance took three millennia. It came from Scotland or northern England in the mid-1600s, when merchants began specializing in fishing tackle. Tree branches were shaved into rods and used with a line of equal length. The line, attached to the tip of the rod, was flopped out, and the rod tip tracked the downstream progress of the swimming fly. Various types of wood were employed, including shaved greenheart, lancewood, hazel, willow, and hickory. Anglers used whatever species of wood was at hand.

In the mid-1850s, Samuel Phillippe from Easton, Pennsylvania, created the biggest innovation in fly fishing up to that point: the fly rod, which he handmade using six bamboo strips. Not satisfied with Phillippe's method, other rod makers created rods from four and eight strips, but the six-strip had staying power and is the standard seen today. Bamboo rods, more commonly known as cane rods, are still made by hand and are expensive. They are favored by some anglers for their sensitive feel and historically romantic characteristics. The best cane comes from the Gulf of Tonkin, the northern arm of the South China Sea. Master rod makers take several days to create a single cane rod, and those makers who are in great demand may have as much as a two-year waiting list for their creations.

Sometime after World War II, fiberglass became popular for fly rod construction. It wasn't the hollow rod we know today, but a solid blank that was square or round in cross-section. This solid form was necessary because fiberglass at that time had a much lower modulus than bamboo and would not recover as quickly because it was too flexible.

An engraving of "gentlemen" anglers fly fishing on the frontispiece of *The British Angler; or, A Pocket-companion for Gentlemen-fishers*, by John Williamson, 1740.

In the 1950s, the fishing rod company Fenwick® developed a thin-walled, hollow fiberglass rod that flexed more like the traditional bamboo rods. They did this by laying up longitudinal lengths of glass fibers, wrapping them around a form, and heating them in an oven. This process is still used these days for modern rod blanks.

In the early 1970s, graphite came out of the aerospace field and into fly rod technology. It remains the most-used material for fly rod manufacturing. The Orvis® Company, which was already a respected manufacturer of cane rods, became a leader in this technology. This worked out well, because prime bamboo was becoming difficult to find and Orvis wanted to maintain its reputation for quality.

Since then, other materials, such as boron and titanium, have been introduced but they have not remained. In order to capture a different market segment, some manufacturers are heading in an old direction—while they used to promote the theory that fiberglass was superior to bamboo, they are now claiming their new fiberglass rods have the closest action to quality bamboo rods, so it appears we have come nearly full circle.

Even mundane accessories such as cork grips reflect nuances in angler preferences. Some fishers desire grips that are longer or shorter; straight or tapered; larger or smaller diameters. It all depends on personal preferences.

FLY REELS

For thousands of years, anglers accomplished their fishing without the aid of reels. Even in contemporary times it's possible to use a hand line, as was done by Santiago in Ernest Hemingway's *The Old Man and the Sea*.

It's believed the Chinese invented the fishing reel sometime in the fourth century CE. Not until the seventeenth century was mention made in Europe of a wooden "winder" for holding line. By the mid-eighteenth century, reels began to be made for specific types of fishing, including fly fishing. The use of a reel, capable of holding extra line, meant that fishers could cast longer distances.

Near the end of the 1800s, modern metallurgy permitted a switch from wooden reels to lightweight metal fly reels. The desired characteristics included large line capacity and a "drag" system that could be used to control the rate at which a fish could pull line from the reel.

Many of the first reels had solid sides. Before long, using stampings to produce perforated side plates made reels lighter in weight. Such manufacturing methods produced inexpensive reels that most fly fishers could afford. Despite these industrial innovations, some fly fishers preferred handmade reels by Edward vom Hofe, Hiram Lewis Leonard, Benjamin Meek, and others.

Modern mass-produced reel choices range from cast aluminum, plastics, and graphite to machined aluminum. These reels can be had for from less than a hundred up to several hundred dollars.

A few contemporary reelsmiths continue to offer handmade reels that can cost thousands of dollars and require a wait time of several months, or even years, for delivery. These models demonstrate metalwork at its finest, with precision gears and drag systems that would be the envy of fine watchmakers.

A collection of antique reels.

Although many believe the purpose of a reel is simply to hold fly line, its size and weight helps to balance the rod's feel in hand and make the act of casting seem effortless. Here, a variety of reels.

FLY LINES AND LEADERS

In the not-so-recent eighteenth century, the line and leader (for connecting the hook to the line) were both made from one material—typically braided horsetail hair. Horsehair is rot-proof and lasts so long that lines and leaders were passed from father to son. By braiding or twisting the hair, fishers could reduce some fibers and produce a tapered leader. The thick end of the line was tied to the top of the rod and was of equal length to the rod: around 10 feet (3 m).

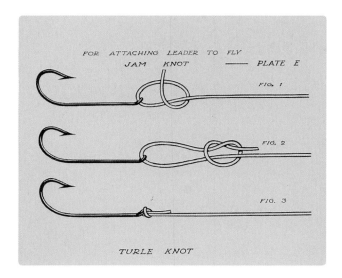

In the early 1800s, line makers began mixing horsehair with silk to increase the line's strength. By the mid-1800s, lines were made of oil-soaked silk. These lines were woven with a hollow core, and they remained unchanged for nearly one hundred years.

In the 1950s, nylon was used for weaving hollow-core fly lines so they would float. Today, nylon-core lines are coated with a PVC covering, and in this way they float without the need for oiling, as was the case with silk lines. Modern fly lines come in numerous profiles to meet a wide range of fly fishing needs. Specific performance lines have weight molded in various configurations so they sink at particular rates to meet underwater fly fishing needs. One-weight lines, the lightest, are used for extremely small flies and short casts. Fifteen-weight lines are used in saltwater fishing where large, heavy flies are the norm.

As hollow, woven silk lines became common, another change occurred. Silk gut, from the silk worm, began to be used as a single-strand leader to connect the fly and the line. Silk gut leaders had to be kept wet or they would dry rot. In 1938, DuPont® invented nylon, and it became the primary material for fly leaders and is still in use for that purpose.

Modern leaders are tapered to specific diameters. Running a level piece of monofilament through a set of graduated cutting dies, each finer than the last, makes the desired final diameter. This yields a leader that is tapered from thick to thin without the necessity for knots. Moreover, selecting different dies can create different profiles of tapers. Tippets of 4-pound (1.8-kg) test are ideal for trout, while heavier tippets of 20-pound (9-kg) test are used for northern pike.

Opposite, top: Detail from a diagram on attaching leaders to a fly, from *Trout Fly-Fishing in America*, by Charles Zibeon Sourhard, 1914.

Opposite, bottom and above: Fly lines come in every color of the rainbow. A wide variety of profiles provide for different allocations of weight. Lines with weight distributed toward the front end are capable of casting heavy flies, while lines with finer front tapers deliver the fly with minimum disturbance when the line lands on the water.

HOW TO TIE A FLY

Many people assume black magic is required to turn feathers into fishing flies. For many years, commercial fly tyers encouraged this misconception as a means to sustain their business. Countless contemporary fly fishers continue to think the skills involved are beyond their abilities, and they purchase their needs from fly shops. As fly fishing became more popular following World War II, more fly tying instruction was made available to aspiring tyers. Organizations such as Trout Unlimited and the International Federation of Fly Fishers offered tying instruction to their members. More recently, the Internet provided instruction in every type of fly tying.

The three tyers featured on these pages represent a cross section of tying specialties: warm water flies, trout flies, and saltwater flies.

SUE POST

I started tying in the mid-1970s because my husband, Rich, asked me to. I like to sew and do crafts, but I never realized how much I would love it. I asked Elsie and Harry Darbee if they would teach me, and they agreed. My children, Tracey and Richard, were young, so they came with me for my lessons. I tied flies and they played with the dog. I tied flies for Elsie and Harry in exchange for materials, so I could tie flies for my husband. Then I decided that I should fly fish too, since I was tying all these flies. I like to make and create my own patterns because you are limited only by your own imagination. You can throw just about anything on a hook and fake out a fish to eat it.

I really enjoy showing others how to tie. I started out with my children. Tracey's and Richard's flies are still in my "special" box. Then I showed my son-in-law, Ron, how to tie. He is very good at it. Many customers ask me questions while I tie flies in our shop, Fur, Fin & Feather Sport, in Livingston Manor, New York.

One of my fondest memories is of when I was given the privilege to go into Livingston Manor High School and show them how flies are the abstract of the realities they were being taught. We have the famous Willowemoc Creek flowing right through town and next to the school, and there was trout in the classroom. The children were so excited to see how a few materials wound on a hook look like insects. I really love tying and fishing, especially with my family. It is a great gift all can enjoy. What memories await those who look around, take a deep breath, and enjoy all that life has to give.

Sue Post is a co-owner of the Fur, Fin & Feather Sport Shop in Livingston Manor, New York.

Tying a Traditional Catskill Dry Fly: The Hair-Wing Gray Fox

1. Placing a size 12 hook in the vise and winding a thread base that will prevent materials from sliding out of place.

2. Measuring wings of calf tail, selected for its floatability, durability, and visibility on the water.

3. Tying the calf tail fibers down.

4. Dividing the wings, tying a tail of ginger hackle fibers, and wrapping a gray fur body.

5. Tying in a grizzly and light ginger hackle.

8. Winding the ginger hackle.

6. Trimming the hackle stem.

9. Whip-finishing the thread to prevent it from unraveling.

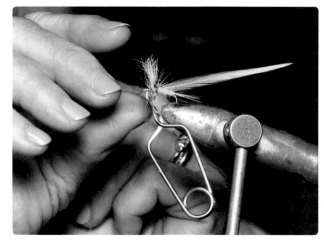

7. Winding the first hackle around the hook and wings.

10. The finished hair-wing gray fox fly.

OWEN MCCAIN

I started fishing with my father when I was three years old, and I've loved it ever since. Nothing in this world brings me as much joy as fighting a bluefish on a fly rod.

I started tying flies when I was four. It was just an experiment with a bunch of feathers on a hook. Shortly after, I was no longer sitting on my father's lap to make ties but was instead creating innovative patterns in my mind. I began testing the details I was experimenting with and studied fish on my own time. What colors look good to me? What colors look good to the fish? What materials look best in the water? I tested flies in my bathtub (which did not sit well with my mother).

My biggest influence is professional fly designer Bob Popovics, because he also likes to experiment with materials and create new patterns. My dad owns River Bay Outfitters in Baldwin, New York, so it was easy getting into the International Fly Tying Symposium and spending time with Bob. From Bob I learned about what materials do in the water, how sparse materials can be, etc. After Bob gave me a lesson, my tying skills have exploded. I now make new patterns simply by looking at materials and knowing exactly how to make the best use of them.

Owen McCain is a competitive fly tyer from Baldwin, New York.

Tying a Flat-Wing Surf Candy

Materials for tying a Flat-Wing Surf Candy.

1. Preparing a Mustad® size 8 stainless steel hook. Stainless is preferred because it will stand up to repeated use in saltwater.

2. Winding a thread base of Danville Ultra Fine Monofilament thread over the hook shank to prevent materials from sliding out of place.

3. Measuring synthetic Steve Farrar's SF Flash for the tail.

6. Tying a length of pearl Bill's Bodi Braid in at the bend.

4. Tying SF fiber in at the bend to prevent fouling on the retrieve.

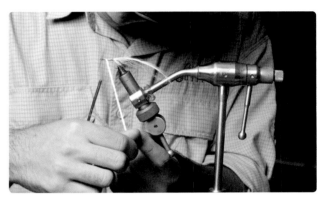

7. Wrapping the braid forward to the hook eye, making the body.

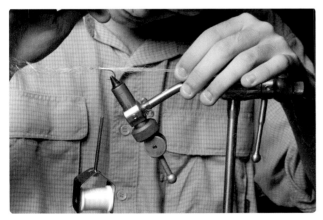

5. Tying a natural white rooster hackle in flat at the bend, which makes it visible from above and below.

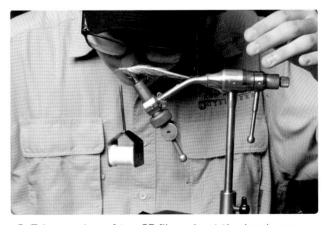

8. Tying a wing of tan SF fibers in at the hook eye.

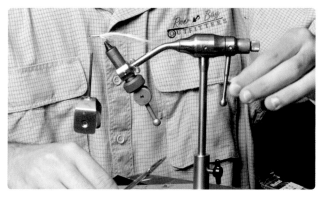

9. Attaching pair of Clear Cure Eyes to the base of the wing. Eyes are favored by tyers because they act as a trigger for the predator fish, who are accustomed to seeing baitfish with eyes.

10. Applying Solarez UV resin to hold all fibers and eyes in their correct, natural positions.

11. Curing the resin with a UV light. Curing hardens the resin and reinforces the fly.

12. A finished Flat-Wing Surf Candy ready for fishing.

LEE WEIL

When I began tying flies in the early '80s, I didn't realize how much it would change my life. After winning a fly tying contest put on by Orvis, I began selling flies and subsequently began teaching classes. It's very gratifying to see a student develop their skills and to pass on techniques that are specific to you as a tyer. You develop a certain way of doing things, and your students benefit from your experience. The passion for tying doesn't always transmit, but when it does, you become kindred spirits.

Unlike many other activities where competition exists, fly tying artists are usually willing to share their knowledge. Even in cases where they do not speak the same language as you. I met a tyer who spoke no English while tying at an international event, yet we were able to communicate through hand signals as he conveyed his technique for creating his nymph pattern.

I am most grateful to those tyers who coached me along the way: Tom Baltz, Bob Lindquist, Jay "Fishy" Fullum, and many others too numerous to mention. Every tyer I know has mentors, and in turn we become mentors to the next generation, as, sadly, the former ones pass on. I feel truly blessed to share this unique art and continue the heritage of the sport.

Lee Weil is a professional fly tyer who designs and sells ties, teaches classes on the art of tying, and competes in tying contests around the world.

Tying a Flatfish Deer-Hair Bass Bug

1. Setting a bronze hook in the vise. Bronze is preferred because it holds up well to large fish.

2. Setting the tail of marabou and flash.

3. Securing the tail with several turns of thread.

4. Positioning the first bucktail bundle. Bucktail hair is hollow, so it floats the fly for long periods of time.

5. Flaring and spinning chartreuse deer hair on top and white underneath because most baitfish have a white belly.

6. Stacking along the hook shank and finishing the body at the hook eye.

7. Trimming into a flat shape, so it will look like an injured baitfish floating on the surface—an easy meal for a predator fish.

8. Completing the trimming while protecting the tail.

9. A razor is used for cleanup.

10. The finished flatfish deer-hair bass bug.

PART TWO

THE FLIES

*"O, Sir, doubt not that Angling is an art; is it not an art to
deceive a Trout with an artificial fly?"*

—Izaak Walton, The Compleat Angler, 1655

ATLANTIC SALMON AND STEELHEAD FLIES

Atlantic salmon flies, the most colorful of all the fly types, have a 250-year history. They were first created in the United Kingdom when the British Empire stretched around the world and so had access to materials from all over the globe.

The first mention of angling for Atlantic salmon appeared in the 1496 *Treatyse on Fysshynge wyth an Angle* by Dame Juliana Berners. It also appeared in Izaak Walton's *The Compleat Angler*, which was published in 1653 and then expanded two years later. However, the first mention of specific patterns for salmon was in James Chetham's 1681 book, *The Angler's Vade Mecum*, in which he compares simple patterns to what we now refer to as "full dressed" patterns.

It is believed that angling for Atlantic salmon was not popular before the nineteenth century. Around that time, the number of books on Atlantic salmon flies began to grow and many specific patterns became known as "classics" due to their effectiveness for producing a strike by salmon returning from the ocean. These classic patterns can require thirty or more different materials. A small group of fly tyers dedicate themselves to reproducing these classic patterns in both materials and methods. A sample is shown in this volume; the work of Paul Martin and Edward Muzeroll (see pages 36–38 and 39–43) represents this enthusiasm for sustaining the tradition of classic Atlantic salmon patterns.

The origin of the classic hairwing salmon fly patterns is believed to have begun sometime during the 1800s. They were likely designed to replace the multi-feather wing with one made of hair.

This substitution was probably made to provide greater action or movement when the fly was in the water. It is also possible that scarcity of the original feather wing materials necessitated the change to the more accessible hairs. Author Joseph D. Bates Jr., in his book *Atlantic Salmon Flies and Fishing*, described hair wings as "mobile while many of the feather wings are stiff. They breathe and pulsate in the current, and act alive. They are juicily translucent while many of the feather-wings are opaque."

Evolution continued and salmon flies were developed for Pacific as well as Atlantic salmon. In addition, other species of anadromous fish (born in freshwater, migrate to saltwater, and return to freshwater to spawn) such as steelhead are targeted by fly fishers. With the advent of synthetic materials, patterns of a wider variety of colors are possible and they provide a shine not seen in natural materials.

Often, one's first impression of traditional Atlantic salmon flies is a myriad of colors. Closer inspection reveals intricate turns of silver or gold wire overlaying sections of silk thread. The distance between each turn of wire and the exact shade of silk are defined by the pattern's originator and contemporary tyers revel in the details. The Atlantic salmon patterns shown on the following pages give testament to the tyer's dedication to this tradition.

An illustration of the Shannon fly from *The Book of the Salmon*, by Edward Fitzgibbon and Andrew Young, 1850.

C. Rex and Blue Beard

Tied by Mike Algar

The C. Rex above is a variation of a typical intruder-style steelhead fly. The intruder was invented in the early 1990s for Alaskan salmon. Jerry French, Ed Ward, and Scott Howell are generally credited with originating this style of fly for targeting Pacific anadromous fish. Since that time, it has become a style rather than a specific fly. The advantage of this style is that it allows a large fly to be fashioned without the use of a big, heavy hook. This is accomplished by wiring two smaller hooks in tandem, one behind the other. The extra-long materials, tied in on the front hook, extend back and cover both hooks, giving the appearance of a large baitfish. Because there is no weight added to this fly, it is easy to cast for steelhead all day.

The C. Rex gets its appeal through the use of polar bear hair, rhea and Lady Amherst pheasant feathers, and soft mallard flank feathers. Mike Algar, a professional guide who runs Freestone Fly Fishers, Ltd. in Calgary, Alberta, named it for its color, cyan. Mike started fishing after his family relocated to banks of the famous Bow River in Calgary in the early '80s. He has been a full-time fly fishing guide on the Bow and in southern Alberta for the last eleven years and has been fly tying both personally and commercially for the last sixteen.

The Blue Beard bridges the gap between tiny wet flies and huge intruder-type flies used for steelhead. Its design allows it to be cast on a Spey rod, which are from 13 to 15 feet (4 to 4.5 m) long and designed for long casts on big rivers. Blue Beard's main job is to fish for steelhead in low, clear water from Idaho and the Olympic Peninsula in Washington State to the upper Skeena River system in British Columbia, Canada.

Corps Nymph

Tied by Mark H. V. Corps

Who doesn't love the image of early Atlantic salmon fishers swinging a multicolored full dressed salmon pattern over resting Atlantic salmon? Casting across and letting a fly swing down does catch lots of Atlantic salmon, but it is not infallible. For those times when it's not working, "minor tactics," including nymphing, can save the day.

Seventeen years ago, Mark H. V. Corps was introduced to the "Czech style" of deep nymph fishing. It worked well for trout and grayling, and after hooking several Atlantic salmon, he realized nymphs are effective on Atlantics—something renowned angler Frank Sawyer (1906–1980) had learned over half a century earlier. The Corps Nymph is technically a stalking bug, which is how it was described by Sawyer.

It wasn't until ten years ago that Mark intentionally fished his stalking bugs for Atlantics. While fishing the Delphi fishery in Ireland, Mark saw several salmon holding in 6 to 8 feet (1.8 x 2.4 m) of water. After switching to a beadhead nymph he hooked one.

Mark says, "To be honest, this was a revelation to me. For a couple of seasons I used the nymphs very successfully. However, trundling heavy flies down a rocky river bed proved expensive in flies. Taking advantage of the water clarity, it slowly dawned on me over a couple of seasons, I could try to stalk these fish. This proved challenging as well as exciting, but importantly productive too (and cheaper on flies).

"As one can imagine it requires creeping in a heron-like manner along the bank. On spotting a fish, the fly needs to be presented carefully and as close as possible to the fish's nose.

"No doubt nymphing and stalking are techniques that the majority of salmon anglers have never seriously tried. However, for me there are now numerous fisheries I would not fish without taking my nymphs with me."

Three Steelhead Flies: Peekaboo Purple, Sleestak Sculpin, and Blue Winter

Tied by Bill Litz

Steelhead and rainbow trout are thought to be the same fish, but rainbow are found only in freshwater while steelhead spend up to two years in the ocean and then return to the big rivers of their birth to spawn. Unlike most Pacific salmon, steelhead (*Oncorhynchus mykiss*) can survive spawning and spawn for multiple years. They average 8 to 11 pounds (3.5 to 5 kg) and can reach 40 pounds (18 kg).

The Peekaboo Purple (center) is Bill Litz's original design. It is a Spey fly, a style originated by Scottish Atlantic salmon fishers on the River Spey in the mid-1800s. They are characterized by a long, flowing hackle attached to the hook by wrapping the feathers around the hook shank. Bill uses it for spring steelhead and migrating landlocked Atlantic salmon in the Great Lakes tributaries.

The Sleestak Sculpin (left) was born of love for the traditional feather-wing streamer patterns. This fly has a great profile when wet and gives more movement than a traditional feather-wing streamer. It works well in slow currents when swinging for steelhead and when trolled at slow speeds from a kayak.

Bill's Blue Winter (right) is a variation on the zonker pattern. Zonkers have a wing of soft fur, often rabbit, tied to the hook shank at the head and tail. It's a great winter steelhead fly and as pleasing to the fisherman's eye as the fish's.

Bill was so involved with trout fishing that through his middle school and high school days he earned the nickname "the trout" from his classmates. Forty years later, and for the past ten years, Bill ties mostly steelhead and salmon flies and searches for the definitive fly that will unfailingly tempt the often temperamental steelhead.

Jock Scott

Tied by Paul Martin

Arguably the most famous salmon fly of all time, the Jock Scott was invented in 1845 by Scottish fishing guide Jock Scott. When tied according to the original dressing, it requires nearly thirty elements (depending on which "original list" you believe), including silk threads and feathers. Because the British Empire spread around the world, there was an abundance of exotic bird species to choose from, including the blue chatterer (more commonly knowns as the blue jay) and the blue-and-yellow macaw.

In the early 1900s fly tyers from Limerick began incorporating many more colors into their patterns. At first, such creations were scoffed at by hidebound tyers. They changed their minds, though, when the colorful creations proved their success across Great Britain and beyond.

Paul Martin of Auburn, Maine, has been dressing classic and creative salmon flies since the 1980s. He started fishing for salmon in the Fish and St. John Rivers in northern Maine and thought dressing up his own flies would save him money and reduce his disappointment from losing so many fished flies on the rocky bottoms of both these rivers. What started out as a hobby quickly developed into a passion to learn the history of salmon fishing and flies. Using vintage books that contained original patterns as guides, he gathered the required antique hooks and authentic feathers to dress historic flies. In the mid-'90s he won the Maine Artist Fellowship for several of his flies. Since then, he has truly appreciated being able to correspond with other fly dressers from across the globe and exchange some of his flies for a few historical books, exotic dressing materials, and others' works of art.

The colorful Britannia salmon fly, illustrated in Fitzgibbon's and Young's *The Book of the Salmon.*

Recently, his very close friend Alvaro Lopez Jr. sent him many vintage hooks, which Paul has started to rework in order to better suit his personal style of hooks and sizes to complement his fly dressing. Being able to dress his flies on these hooks has helped to reduce the cost of his flies, which has in turn allowed him to be better able to gift some of his flies to those who have crossed his path or made a contribution to his life. Without a doubt, dressing salmon flies has enriched that life. Paul's Jock Scott is dressed with all authentic materials, and he used his own homemade hook. For another of his flies, see page 38.

Green Highlander

Tied by Paul Martin

The Green Highlander was first mentioned in 1885 and attributed to a Mr. Grant. As was the case at that time, certain Atlantic salmon flies were believed to be more effective on some rivers than on others. The Green Highlander was categorized as a River Ness fly. The River Ness flows from the northern end of Loch Ness in Scotland, through Loch Dochfour, northeast to Inverness, into Beauly Firth, to Moray Firth, and out to the North Sea.

Given the large number of materials required for classic salmon patterns, it should come as no surprise that salmon fly tyers argue over minute details such as which material is superior for tiny segments of the fly. In this case, some prefer flat silver tinsel for the tag while others claim silver thread and yellow floss are more effective for attracting salmon. Whether and how salmon can even discern the almost insignificant difference is debatable. Paul's Green Highlander is dressed with authentic materials and his own homemade hook. For another of his flies, see pages 36–37.

Dunc's Delight

Tied by Edward "Muzzy" Muzeroll

Dunc's Delight was designed by Edward Muzeroll of Sidney, Maine, in memory of the late Warren Duncan. Muzzy said, "Warren was one of those bigger-than-life characters. If you don't know of Warren, then it's worth doing some web research." Warren Duncan (1948–2007) tied tens of thousands of classic salmon flies and influenced, on a personal basis, the development of creative skills for numerous contemporary salmon tyers.

Muzzy, a designer for Bath Iron Works who travels to ports all over the world to assess ships for upcoming additions and changes, wanted to project size in the fly to represent the larger-than-life person that Warren was. Like the feathers used in this fly—from the Indian crow as a tail veiling, to the dark blue cotinga, and all the way to the cheeks of resplendent quetzal and riflebird, and finally the throat of banded gymnogene—Warren was like all these materials. He was bold, colorful, inviting, and most of all, like the banded gymnogene throat, Warren was a very soft and gentle man. RIP.

For more flies by Muzzy, see pages 40–43.

Bogdan Special
Tied by Edward "Muzzy" Muzeroll

Muzzy's creativity is in immense supply, and it shows in how his Bogdan Special fly came to be. Stanley Bogdan (1918–2011) was the master of hand-tooled fly reels. This Nashua, New Hampshire, resident lived to be 92 and, at age 91, he caught a 32-pound salmon. His obituary in the *New York Times* noted that Stan's reels could only be had after a wait that could be as long as four years. Being hand-tooled, only one hundred were completed each year. You could expect to pay $1,500 for the smallest trout reel and about $2,400 for the biggest salmon reel.

Muzzy recalled, "After meeting Stanley Bogdan on the Atlantic salmon rivers of the Gaspé [Peninsula in Quebec] and at fly fishing shows, and after getting to know him, I was thinking I should design a fly with him in mind. It was not until after his death that I finally set down to work on one.

"If you knew Stanley, you know he was a character and full of life even toward the end. I happened to be looking through an issue of *Art of Angling Journal* when I saw a fly that inspired this pattern/style.

"I choose feathers that I think Stan would have liked. He was a bit flashy like the eyes of the Malay peacock feathers and the dark blue cotinga. He was also subtle like the main wing of blue and red macaw. Stanley had a bit of white hair I represented by the light-colored body veiling of toucan."

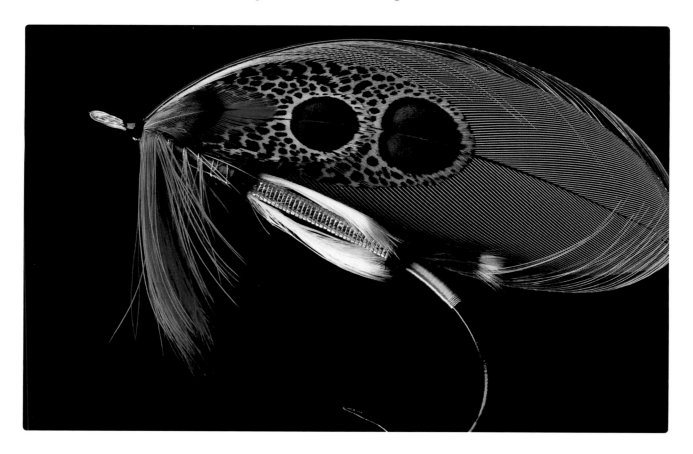

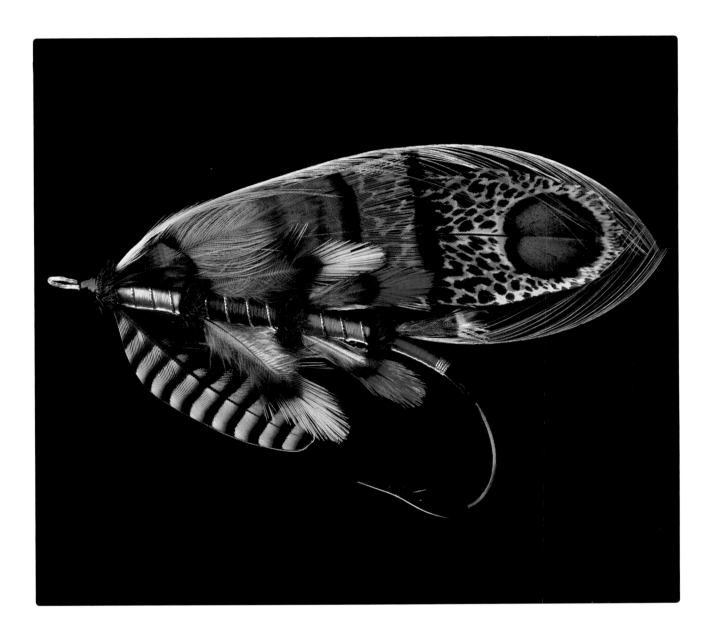

Treasure Island

Tied by Edward "Muzzy" Muzeroll

Inspiration comes to Muzzy from many places. Often, it is the result of a personal experience, as is the case with his Treasure Island.

"Treasure Island was designed with the tropical islands I have visited in mind: Hawaii and the Seychelle Islands. The darker colors represent the vegetation on the islands, and the shades of blue represent the water and sky of the tropics. I used two species of cotinga, Indian crow, riflebird, and Eurasian jay." These species may not be familiar to many outside the cadre of salmon fly tyers. A visit to YouTube will show these beautiful birds in action.

For more flies by Muzzy, see pages 39 and 42–43.

Johnnie Walker

Tied by Edward "Muzzy" Muzeroll

There is a set of acknowledged "classic" full dressed Atlantic salmon flies. Many tyers devoted themselves to replicating them, and only them, as a way of preserving this art. They seek out the original materials, many of which have become extinct or at least difficult to find. Other tyers also dedicate themselves to creating works of art in the style of the classics. Muzzy gives some insight into how that creative process happens and turns into flies like his Johnnie Walker. "I must admit this was a fly I envisioned while at work one day. I sometimes allow my mind to wander. In my mind, I go through my inventory of materials and try to mix and match things, to create a fly that I find appealing.

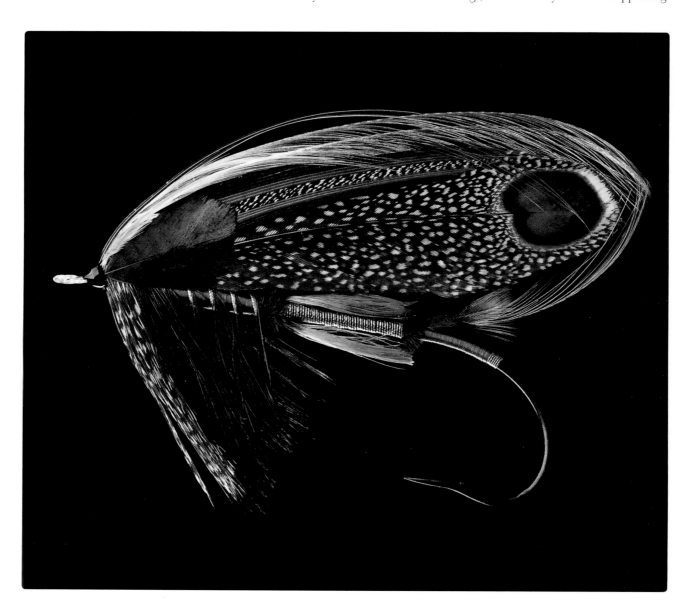

So, after a day at work, I came home and hauled out the materials that make up the Johnnie Walker.

"After finishing the fly I had no name for it. But, as I took another sip of some Johnnie Walker Green, it hit me. I saw earthy tones, and all the speckle of the main wing of gray peacock pheasant, the speckle of the kori bustard in the married wing over the main wing, and the speckle in the throat of gray peacock hackle. All the speckles reminded me of the spice notes in the wee dram I was enjoying."

Muzzy added, "I have met so many great people who I now consider friends . . . just due to the fact that I tie classic salmon flies. I tied at shows on the East Coast for about ten years but have gotten away from it. I have held classes on tying classics and really enjoy sharing what I have learned from trial and error, and from all my fellow tyers." For more flies by Muzzy, see pages 39–41.

Two Classic Salmon Flies: Rory and St. Lawrence

Tied by Ted Patlen

Ted Patlen has won seven world fly tying championships and gives fly tying demonstrations around the globe. He is a traditionalist who tries to use the materials and techniques that were in use during the time the patterns were developed.

Of interest on these two full dressed salmon patterns is the silkworm gut "eye." Up until the eighteenth century, horsetail hair was used to attach the fly to the line. Silkworm gut, literally the inside of silkworms, was discovered to be a better material for this purpose. Blind-eyed hooks (without eyes) needed a device to make the connection and a loop of gut was lashed to the hook shank to make the connection possible.

The larger of these two patterns (bottom) is the Rory. It is described in Sir Herbert Maxwell's 1898 book, *Salmon and Sea Trout: How to Propagate, Preserve, and Catch Them in British Waters*. Flies tied on huge hooks were typically used in the early season and flooded rivers. What's interesting is that the recipe for the wing is very uncomplicated. Except for one or two components, the rest of the wing is defined as "strips of any feather long enough." So much for exactness.

Ted's smaller pattern, the St. Lawrence, is typical of the classic look of 1880s' salmon flies. He re-forged the hook to get the look he wanted, as the hooks originally used in the 1880s are rare and many styles are no longer available. The solution is to take an existing hook and re-forge it to the specifications of the original hook design. For more flies by Ted Patlen, see pages 76–77, 78–79, and 118.

Golden Demon

Tied by Justin Sanders

Justin Sanders, from Vancouver, British Columbia, is a professional fly tyer. Here, he has tied two variations of the Golden Demon. As can be seen, the materials are identical in both flies. The only exception is that one is tied on a hook shank while the other is tied on a tube.

Tube flies have an interesting history. In the nineteenth century, native North Americans used "flies" tied on hollow quills to fish for West Coast Pacific salmon. The method disappeared from the record until the 1930s, when it first appeared in print.

In 1945, Winnie Morawski, a fly dresser with Charles Playfair & Co. in Aberdeen, Scotland, was credited with this style. Hers was tied on fragile turkey quills. Soon after, William Michie, a British doctor, replaced the turkey quill with much stronger surgical tubing. The hook's shank is tied to the leader and then the hook is drawn up into the tube. In an independent discovery, Pacific Coast salmon fishers in Oregon and Washington discovered earlier native North American tube flies and since 1945, these patterns have been adopted in the United States.

Tube flies were originally created as long-bodied trolling flies. Since that time, they have also become casting flies. In addition, many existing fly patterns have been transformed into tube flies. Advantages of tube flies are many: the fly is free to slide up the leader during the fight, so the fly is not destroyed; shorter shank hooks can be used, resulting in less leverage and fewer break-offs during the fight; and if a hook breaks or becomes dull, the rest of the fly is reusable.

Hair-Wing Salmon Flies

Tied by Barry Stokes

The art of early traditional Atlantic salmon flies is kept alive by a small group of dedicated tyers, but evolution is a certainty. When some materials became scarce, traditional salmon tyers turned to "hair-wing" patterns that kept the form and color combinations found in the original patterns.

Another advancement is also shown in this tie: the use of synthetic living fiber (SLF). Being a synthetic, it has a sheen not found in natural materials and the colors are unlimited and vibrant.

Barry Stokes, from Victoria, British Columbia, began tying in the 1980s. What started as a hobby soon turned into an obsession. As Barry progressed, he found himself dabbling in the art of fly tying, and soon after that he was teaching classes. This also led to working part time in a local fly shop and supplying a few other shops with flies. His friends were so impressed with his work that they asked him to tie some for fundraisers. These were mounted in shadow boxes and auctioned off. Other materials captured Barry's attention until he began tying these hair-wing SLF flies again when he rediscovered them twenty years later.

Since then, his accomplishments have been widely acknowledged and his work has appeared in many fly fishing magazines and fly tying books. He was also honored as the first recipient of the Jack Shaw Fly Tying Award, presented by the British Columbia Federation of Fly Fishers in 2001.

TROUT FLIES

Trout flies are the most commonly tied patterns because the majority of fly fishers fish for trout. Some patterns are so impressively lifelike that one waits for them to fly away. As imitations of natural insects, they are unimaginably delicate. The enlarged images on the following pages will make this detail obvious.

As discussed on page 4, the earliest written record of fly fishing (and tying) comes from Roman author Claudius Aelianus. Around 200 CE, Aelianus described the length of the rod and the red wool, feathers, and other colorful materials used to create a fly that would attract fish. His description continues to explain that there is a natural insect the trout feed upon, and when that insect is on the water, the Macedonian fly will fool the "spotted fish." While Aelianus's text is generally accepted as the earliest description of fly fishing, writings from the Shang dynasty in China, four thousand years ago, also describe an artificial fly used to catch fish. Whether fly tying has existed for eighteen hundred or four thousand years, what is certain is that it requires a true skill to create such ephemeral art.

Some trout patterns strive for anatomical exactness of the natural insect they imitate. Others rely on the illusion of subsurface life-forms, especially their movements in the water. Yet others still look nothing like any life-form on this, or presumably any other, planet. Their function is to attract the attention of opportunistically feeding trout.

LIGHT
COLORED FLIES

MEDIUM
COLORED FLIES

DARK
COLORED FLIES

(2) PROFESSOR

(4) BLACK GNAT

(1) COACHMAN

(5) BROWN HACKLE

(3) ROYAL COACHMAN

(8) COWDUNG

(7) MONTREAL

(6) WHITE MILLER

(9) GRIZZLY KING

(10) SCARLET IBIS

(11) QUEEN OF THE WATERS

(12) SILVER DOCTOR

A plate showing the twelve most popular wet flies used by anglers in the United States in the early twentieth century, from *Trout Fly-Fishing in America,* by Charles Zibeon Sourhard, 1914.

Naturally occurring materials such as feathers, fur, and hair were once the mainstays of fly tying. There were, and are, huge varieties available. When synthetic materials were developed, especially post–World War II, fly tyers began incorporating them into their patterns. Some synthetics outperformed natural materials. For example, holographic tinsel has a reflective quality unmatched in nature.

As hook makers began developing much larger hooks than those initially available, fly patterns could, as necessary, imitate a trout's larger prey. Similarly, the production of small hooks, some as small as this letter *j* allowed tyers to mimic tiny midges, a year-round source of trout food. Contemporary hook manufacturers offer an endless variety of hook shapes intended to provide the foundation for any fly one can imagine.

Most trout flies are tied by fly fishers for their own use, and the patterns need not be too complicated. Some tyers, on the other hand, are professionals, and their creations are in great demand by fishers and collectors alike. Many examples in this volume were created by the finest tyers in the world.

The Norwegian Connection:
Kristin Lavransdatter
and Heggeli Streamer

Tied by Pål Andersen

Many fly fishers make their start as youngsters, but Pål Andersen claims an even earlier start. His parents insist he was conceived during a fishing trip to the Hallingdal, a valley in the mountains of southern Norway. At age eleven, several years after he started fishing, Pål caught his first dry fly trout in the same valley. It was a homecoming, of sorts. Today, Pål is a competitive fly fisherman. He has represented Norway in several World and European Fly Fishing Championships, and he has won individual as well as team championships in Norwegian national competitions several times. But he is likely most proud of his individual European bronze medal in Sunnfjord 2006 because, as of this writing, Pål has the only Norwegian International Medal in fly fishing. He also won the first Norwegian National Championship in one-handed fly-casting. He also has several top-ten placements in the Mustad Scandinavian Open Fly Tying Competition.

The Kristin Lavransdatter (opposite left) was named for the heroine of an early twentieth century trilogy of

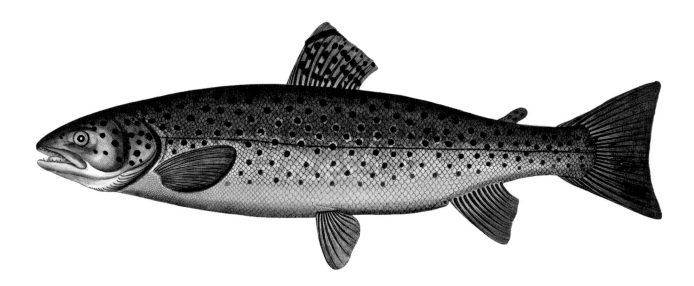

books by Norwegian novelist Sigrid Undset and for a pool in the river Gudbrandsdalslågen. Pål designed this fly in the early 1990s with two universally effective elements: peacock herl for the metallic green body, and a long, soft, variegated wrapped collar that is tied in the round.

Pål's Heggeli Streamer (below right) is a fly based on a very old Norwegian pattern called the Heggeli fly— Heggeli being an area in Oslo with small forest lakes. This fly soon became known as one of the best flies for sea trout and Atlantic salmon. Pål reports it is important that the wing be made from Siberian squirrel.

Top to Bottom

Tied by Jerry Atencio

Although trout are usually opportunists, at times they can be finicky about what they eat. This selective feeding can happen when a particular form of insect stage is prevalent. For example, when mayflies emerge from the water, they are found in very large numbers. This is a survival strategy to insure some will live on to mate and produce future generations. Mayflies live underwater for a year but above the water only for a couple of days. They molt through several submerged stages before hatching on the water's surface into the adult flying stage. Within a day or two after flying away, they molt into the mating and egg-laying stages. A thinner body, longer tails, and almost-clear wings characterize this final transformation.

After seeing to the needs of the next generation, they fall, dead and dying, onto the water's surface in large numbers, providing an easy meal for trout. Before this, though because so much happens underwater, fishers cannot be sure what stages the insects are in at a given time, so they need a full quiver of insect pattern types to draw from if they want to be successful.

Jerry Atencio from New Mexico shows the flies he uses to explore the depths when no flies are showing on the surface. They represent different forms of different insects, but most are subsurface imitations. The hackled fly (lower right) is a dry fly, intended to be fished when dark mayflies are being taken from the river's surface. Others represent various forms of insect stages appearing underwater.

Facocchi Mayfly

Tied by Walter "Wolly" Bayer

This style of fly was seen for the first time more than twenty-five years ago and it was, and still is, called a Facocchi Mayfly. The De Santis brothers Valter and Ennio created this unique style. The brothers are coachbuilders, hence the name *cocchi*, which is "coaches" in Italian.

The fly is not tied around the hook shank, as is the case with most flies. Instead, it's tied around strings of monofilament fishing line and the hook hangs freely under the fly. The advantages are a substantially thinner fly body and a hook that swims under the fly body unweighted. This allows the fly to follow the river's current in a more natural way.

This Facocchi Mayfly was tied by Walter "Wolly" Bayer, who was born in Germany and now lives in Ireland. His home water includes the River Boyne in Leinster, in County Meath. Self-taught, it took him two years to learn the skills required for tying this type of pattern. He now travels around Europe teaching these techniques at fly fishing shows. He also has a fly in the Masters Fly Collection that is bequeathed to the Catskill Fly Fishing Center & Museum. See page 56 for another fly tied by Wolly.

Waggy Tail Sculpin Upside Down

Tied by Walter "Wolly" Bayer

Early-season fishing presents certain challenges. In cold water, fish are lethargic and often settle on the bottoms of rivers. The challenges for the fly fisher are to get a fly deep and fish it slowly, trying to find the fish. When creating his Waggy Tail Sculpin Upside Down (below) for this time of year, Wolly needed a heavy pattern but also wanted a nice, enticing movement. His solution was to adapt a pattern by master fly tyer and expert fisherman Oliver Edwards to meet his own needs.

He rotated the hook so it rides point-up, thereby reducing fouling on the bottom. For extra weight, Wolly used lead dumbbell eyes and extra metal beads under the deer-hair head. The body is made from a strip of trimmed rabbit fur. Dark eyes are tied in place during the forming of the head. Wolly reports catching many brown trout and big pike with this tie, and his best so far was a 24-inch (61-cm) salmon. For another of his flies, see page 55.

Three Old-Timers: Emergent Sparkle Pupa, Jassid, and *Tricorythodes*

Tied by Andrew Bogley

Andrew Bogley, from Hunker, Pennsylvania, is preserving classic, early trendsetting flies. These patterns are small, but they've had a large impact on fly fishing for trout.

From largest to smallest (on opposite page): the Emergent Sparkle Pupa has been around for more than forty years. It was developed by Gary LaFontaine as a caddisfly pattern at a time when mayflies were getting most of the attention. LaFontaine spent a lot of time diving underwater to observe what could not be seen from above. His tying techniques improved fishers' success by employing synthetic materials to imitate the look of emerging caddisflies.

The Jassid was developed by Vince Marinaro in the 1940s. This terrestrial pattern ushered in the era of imitating ultra-small flies that were available to trout during the summer months. This small fly created a demand

for terrestrial beetle patterns that imitate those insects that have fallen into the water. As a result, fishers learned they could be successful through previously unproductive times.

Tricorythodes (tricos) were first identified as a major trout food in the 1950s in spite of their tiny size. However, hook manufacturers did not make hooks small enough to make the diminutive flies until the late '60s. The "spinner" stage (white wings held flat on the water) is the most import stage, because that is when the flies lay their eggs and die in huge masses. The abundant fall of tiny bugs invites voracious feeding by trout.

Over the years, Andrew Bogley has become a self-taught and dedicated fly fisherman specializing in the pursuit of fly fishing spring creeks such as Pennsylvania's LeTort Spring Run. As a fly tyer, writer, and amateur aquatic entomologist, he spends most of his time fishing the limestone streams of central and south-central Pennsylvania.

Mayfly Spinner

Tied by Corey Cabral

This mayfly spinner pattern, by Corey Cabral of southwestern Ontario, Canada, is tied using synthetic materials. He wanted a fly that was easy to tie, buoyant, would ride well in the water, and would imitate a rusty spinner or spent mayfly dun. The body of the fly is tied using a synthetic quill material that is lightweight and durable. A synthetic fur-dubbed thorax sits next to synthetic mayfly wings tied in to lie flat on the water's surface.

Corey Cabral is a fanatical angler and professional tyer with the retailer Frosty Fly, which offers realistic fly tying materials and tenkara gear. He has fished for his entire life but did not pick up a fly rod until 2011 and only started tying around 2012. He is interested in tying different styles and types of flies, and he loves trying new patterns and experimenting with new materials. Corey explains, "I love that fly tying has such a deep and rich history rooted in traditional techniques and materials, but at the same time individuals and companies are always innovating and trying to create new materials and techniques to expand the definition of fly tying." He fishes primarily for Great Lakes steelhead but also loves fishing for resident brown and rainbow trout. For more flies by Corey Cabral, see opposite and page 112.

Nymphs

Tied by Corey Cabral

Many of the insects preferred by trout live out their lives crawling underwater among the rocks. Only when they become active, in preparation for hatching, do they expose themselves to the fish.

Corey Cabral investigated this pattern by flipping over rocks in his local rivers, photographing different nymphs, and then imitating them back at the tying vise. Corey said, "These patterns are quick and easy to tie and have gotten lots of attention due to their semi-realistic look. They fall into the new age of fly tying incorporating synthetics and silicone. While some fishermen and tyers look down on this style of tying, the hobby and sport have kept evolving and changing throughout the years."

Emerging Extended Body Mayfly

Tied by Jonathan Charlton

Not all mayflies make it to the river's surface. Many become trapped, never to escape and mate. Jonathan Charlton, from Saskatoon, Saskatchewan, needed a mayfly pattern that imitates a hatching mayfly trapped in the surface tension. Why? Because mayflies that are trapped in the surface tension are an easy meal for fish to capture. Why? Because, those that hatch out normally spend very little time on the water, unlike those imitated by Jonathan's Emerging Extended Body Mayfly.

Here, Jonathan is showing both an emerging, trapped mayfly as well as one that has broken through the surface and is sitting on top waiting for its wings to dry.

Bruce's Dragonfly

Tied by Bruce Corwin

"Show" flies and fishing flies, Bruce Corwin from Boca Raton, Florida, ties them all. He explained, "I love all types of fishing but have spent the last thirty years with a fly rod in hand. As a graphic artist and designer, fly tying was a natural extension of my creative side. It allowed me to stay close to fishing through the winter months.

"This delicate Dragonfly is not intended to be fished but rather to be displayed as an example of creative fly tying. I'm involved in multiple fly fishing and tying groups including The Hudson Valley Fly Fishers, Ray Bergman chapter of TU (Trout Unlimited), and Joan Wulff Fly Fishers. I'm a New York State licensed guide and have tied at numerous fly tying events."

Bodsjöflugan

Tied by Jan Edman

The Bodsjöflugan (Lake Bodsjö fly) was described by Rudolf Hammarström in his 1925 book *Handbok i sportfiske* (*Guide for Game Angling*). He wrote, "This fly has been proven to be excellent for big trout. It's rarely missing from my leader."

Jan Edman, from Sweden, likes to tie old patterns. He also likes to search out the original materials to make his flies authentic.

Jan learned this fly was originally fished in Bodsjön, a private lake in the Swedish mountains, and he had the opportunity to fish there a few years ago. Of course he had to try the Bodsjöflugan, and he did catch trout on it. He reports it was a very great feeling to see that this old pattern still catches fish. The distinctive eye-catching wing is made with blue jay feather.

Jan is very interested in the history of fly tying and fly fishing, not only in Sweden but also in New York's Catskills. He's been there twice and met some great fly tyers and fly fishers. He is the only Swede, so far, who has been a guest fly tyer at the Catskill Fly Fishing Center & Museum.

Fishing Beetle

Tied by Fabrizio Gajardoni

After seeing some beautiful bugs on the Mür River in Austria, Fabrizio Gajardoni of Italy decided to tie some imitations. In 1998, he started by catching beetles and taking them to his tying bench.

The iridescent and brilliant material for the body of this tie is a plastic cloth found on shopping bags in his home city, Rimini. When he first saw this material, he understood immediately it was perfect for his beetles. For the antennae he tied plastic hair, which is very thin and strong, and colored with acrylic paint protected by epoxy.

Since that time, Fabrizio has improved the pattern, trying new materials as he discovers them. Among the best is seal fur, which has the right brilliance and comes in natural colors. He especially loves hot orange because it gives him the best results in every river he fishes. The beetle pattern comes into its own during summer months when terrestrials are the major food source for trout.

Fabrizio is the innovative creator of several fly dressings and is known for his versatility with every type of fly. From dry flies to flies for pike and bass, trout nymphs to saltwater flies, realistic creations to full dressed salmon flies, he is a master at the tying vise. From 1997 to 2003 Fabrizio won two gold, two silver, and four bronze medals in different categories of fly tying competitions at various Mustad Scandinavian Opens.

Oki Kebari

Tied by Daniel Galhardo

This Japanese tenkara fly is known as *kebari* (literally translated as "haired hook"). Flies used in the tenkara fly fishing method are often very simple, as is the method itself, which uses only a rod, line, and fly (see page 4).

The first written mention of tenkara fly fishing was made in 1878 in reference to local commercial fishermen using flies to catch the yamame (a Japanese trout) in the streams near Mount Tate (Tateyama). Tenkara was originally the domain of commercial fishermen in mountainous areas of Japan. They would catch fish and sell them to villagers and innkeepers. That history is important in helping understand tenkara, and ultimately in helping keep fly fishing simple.

Perhaps the most intriguing aspect of tenkara flies is how tenkara anglers will approach their assortment and then the selection of their fly. It is very common to rely on only a couple of variations on one pattern. This is drastically different from the "match-the-hatch" concept taught in Western fly fishing.

In 2008, Daniel Galhardo visited Japan, where he fell in love with the tenkara's uncomplicated nature and decided fly fishers back home needed to learn about it. He founded Tenkara USA, a company that specializes in creating tenkara rods, lines, and flies and sharing the tenkara story. Tenkara USA is the first American company to introduce tenkara outside Japan. Since the inception of Tenkara USA, Daniel has returned to Japan every year to learn more about the method directly from the masters. You can learn more from the comfort of your home by reading Daniel's book, *Tenkara*.

Bee and Dragonfly

Crafted by Fred Hannie

Insects we see every day can take on a new significance when interpreted by a fly tyer. We can't quite fathom how fly tyers are able to incorporate all the details necessary to convince us—and fish—that the fly is not an imitation, but a real insect. There are twenty thousand species of bees buzzing around the world. And there are over three thousand species of dragonflies around the globe. They're found on every continent except Antarctica. However, none of them approach the 30-inch (75-cm) size of their fossilized ancestors.

Fred Hannie, from Lake Charles, Louisiana, crafts realistic details into his work to mimic the fine details of different species. It's not until you see a live specimen side by side with Fred Hannie's lures that you can appreciate the incredible detail Fred captures in his realistic work. His work has appeared on many magazine covers with features inside that give his instructions on creating realistic flies. His book, *Fly Tying with Monofilament*, also shows how he constructs his creations. For more flies by Fred Hannie, see pages 103 and 114.

Case Caddis

Tied by Konstantin "Kody" Karagyozov

Konstantin "Kody" Karagyozov, from Plovdiv, the second-largest city in Bulgaria, is not a professional, high-production fly tyer. He ties for others only upon special request. His are not show flies for display but are fishing flies made from durable materials that nonetheless create realistic fishing flies. He believes it is more satisfying to fish with a good-looking fly. Kody is a cofounder and chairman of his city's fly fishing club, Mayna Fly, which is part of the Bulgarian Fly Fishing Federation.

Kody's developed his Case Caddis because he was bored with all the peeping caddis larva patterns (caddis larvae with only the head peeping out from the case). So he decided to create something that looked more like a real creature but was still designed for fishing. Because the main feature of the cased caddis is the sand case, he used real sand from his favorite river. Not only is the appearance realistic, the weight of the sand allows the fly to sink toward the bottom where the natural cased caddis is found. For more flies by Kody, see opposite and page 104.

Scud

Tied by Konstantin "Kody" Karagyozov

Many of the things that trout eat are exceptionally small. The scud—the genus *Gammarus* that is sometimes called freshwater shrimp—is an aquatic insect that never emerges into a flying insect, so it is available to feeding trout throughout the year. Some varieties are nearly translucent, and their organs can be viewed through their thin exoskeleton.

For Kody, the idea of tying his own imitation of scuds came after he watched a video of Oliver Edwards tying his scud pattern and then fishing with it. In the following years, Kody tried many variations but was never satisfied until he discovered UV resin. This was the missing piece for producing good looking *and* lifelike patterns that have all the features needed for successful fishing.

Troutlands Cicada and Troutlands Smelt

Tied by Martin Langlands

Martin Langlands is from South Island, New Zealand, where he owns Troutlands Guide Service and has led more than 2,600 guiding trips. That's the kind of experience required to consistently take New Zealand's wary brown trout, and his guests come from all around the world to experience New Zealand's legendary fisheries.

Martin started as a commercial fly tyer in the early 1980s with a huge passion for trout fly design and a sense of experimentation. He reports that the Troutlands Cicada is a great summer dry fly for trout in both rivers and lakes. It imitates mostly cicada but is also impressionistic of many terrestrial insects. A few strands of pearl crystal flash are incorporated as suggestions of wings. It is important to make these strands longer than the body but not to add too many strands, as over-flash can spook some of the large, cautious South Island brown trout.

The Troutlands Smelt imitates smelt and many other baitfish and can be used for trout, especially sea run brown trout, but it can also be used for saltwater species that prey upon sprats, smelt, and young baitfish. Martin uses this pattern often in springs near the coast in rivers, lakes, and where rivers enter the ocean for sea run brown trout. There is perhaps no better place to be testing his many patterns on New Zealand's large, wild, and often very clever trout. The most unique feature of this pattern is the widened body that is achieved by cutting an aluminum drink can to shape and gluing it onto the hook. The body is then covered with a wide pearl braid that gives a realistic baitfish appearance and form.

Traditional Feather-Wing Streamers
Tied by Larry Leight

This style of fly, intended to imitate smelt and other bait-fish, was developed in northern Maine in the early 1920s. In profile, this fly shows as a long slender form. The materials used were selected to emphasize color variations found in the natural baitfish.

Traditional feather-wing streamers were used to attract brook trout and landlocked salmon. During the early 1900s, brook trout of up to 10 pounds (4.5 kg) were fairly common. Being large fish, they favored fairly large prey. As a result, these patterns often measured up to 5 inches (12.7 cm) in length.

Larry Leight, from New York, is a modern tyer who is committed to preserving the tradition of feather-wing streamers. His creations are named for the North Branch Moose River and the Sacandaga in Upstate New York, rivers he knows best. Much of Larry's special interest was due to the classic Northeast streamer flies from the Rangeley, Maine, area, created by Carrie Stevens.

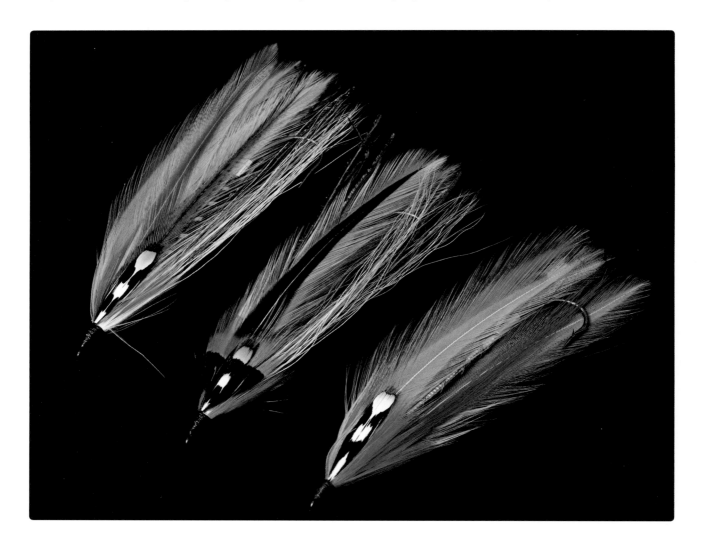

Dave's Mouse

Tied by Dave Matenaer

Dave Matenaer is from Wisconsin and primarily ties flies for fishing. A mouse is not often thought of as trout food but big trout, the kind that come out after dark to feed, want a mouthful.

Dave's Mouse looks real and swims in a lifelike manner. He's also tied a few with legs and feet, to make it look more realistic. However, since most mouse pattern fishing for trout takes place after dark, these extra details might be lost on the fish. However, these additional details give extra confidence to the fly fishers who ply their specialty trade creeping along in the dark as they try to avoid unseen river hazards such as deep water and submerged boulders.

In addition to trout, bass, pike, and carp like to eat a mouse too. These warm-water species are also three of Dave's other favorite species to target. Pike are explosive and will take huge flies on top of the water or at the subsurface. Watching the strike is his favorite part of pike fishing. Carp, on the other hand, can be very skittish and wary. The Great Lakes carp are huge, some exceeding 30 pounds (15 kg).

Dave has been tying since he was ten years old, and after twenty-two years he's still at it. He used to tie at fly fishing expos around the state when he was younger, where he learned techniques from a wide variety of tyers. At each event he would sit next to two different tyers, and since he was a young tyer, they would share anything they could to teach him new techniques.

The Bridge Between Realism and Fishability: Menz's Cicada, Ant, and Blowfly

Tied by Christof Menz

Fly patterns run the range from the suggestive to exact imitations. The former are easy to tie, while the latter are difficult and are often intended to be displayed as show flies. Somewhere in between are realistic fishing flies—more realistic than suggestive show flies but less realistic than precise imitations.

Christof Menz is the founder of the Pro-Guides Flyfishing Company in Austria. He has worked as a full-time, professional guide and course instructor for twenty years. He has lots of experience fly fishing the central European rivers of Austria and Slovenia, but he also loves to fish saltwater Nordic rivers for Atlantic salmon. His favorite spot for trout fishing is the South Island of New Zealand.

Menz's Cicada was a result of research to find out the best pattern for fishing in New Zealand. Trout there really love the perfect silhouette and realistic look presented by Menz's Cicada. His Ant is simple and easy to tie with a nice, realistic look. You can tie this pattern in various sizes and colors to match the ants you commonly find wherever you're fishing. Christof's Blowfly is one of the most important patterns used for fishing on the South Island of New Zealand. The black foam in Christof's fly helps the pattern to float indefinitely.

Hydropsyche Larva

Tied by Tim Morales

Not every fly pattern is ephemeral or even elegant. Some are downright ugly, but that's how they are intended to be. This *Hydropsyche* larva is Tim Morales's version of a crawly thing that lives underwater among the rocks.

The *Hydropsyche* larva is unique among caddisflies because it spins a silk net, or sieve, at the open end of its home, in which it catches its food. This requires the larva to live in streams where the current will carry food into its net. Unfortunately for the *Hydropsyche* larva, the currents that bring it food can also dislodge the larva from the rocks, and it then becomes food for trout.

Tim wanted a realistic pattern that had all the morphological features of a *Hydropsyche* larva and could be fished among rocks without the worry of doing damage to the fly itself. Tim says this is a very durable fly that can catch many fish before needing to be retired.

Tim Morales has been tying flies for just over a year, though his first experience fishing was at the age of four. He was with his grandfather on a small lake near Greenville, Michigan, where he used a fly rod rigged with a worm and a bobber, and caught his first fish, a largemouth bass. He started tying mainly as a way to diversify his fly selection. He is drawn to every type of fly tying, and has dabbled in as many different styles as possible. For more flies by Tim, see pages 74 and 117.

Mosquito

Tied by Tim Morales

Most fly fishers swat at these pests and wonder why they exist. Some realistic fly tyers see them and wonder, why not try them?

This mosquito was inspired by master tyer Peder Wigdell (another contributor to this book; see pages 90–91) who tied something similar. This fly is purely meant to be an artistic piece and would likely not hold up well to fishing. It is a life-size replica and is tied on a #16 grub hook. Look closely and you'll see that the abdomen is red, just as it would be after feeding. For more flies by Tim Morales, see pages 73 and 117.

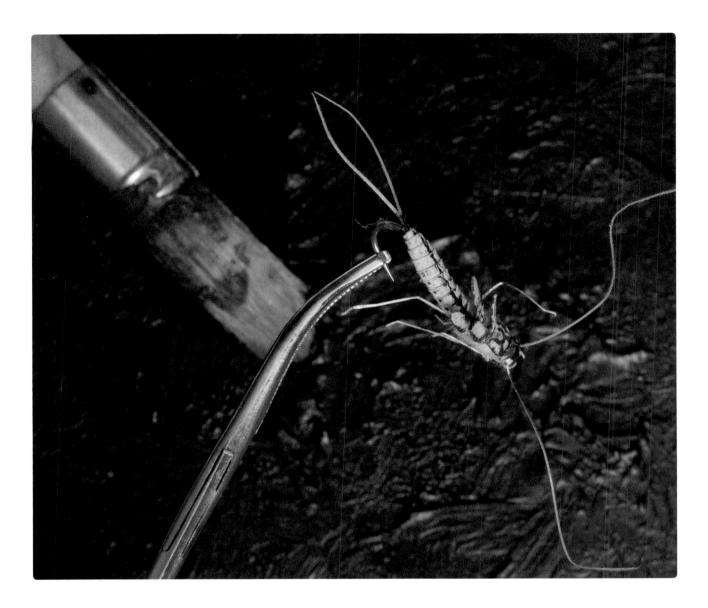

Swimming Stonefly Nymph

Tied by Wirianto Ng

Wirianto Ng is the first fly casting instructor from Indonesia to be certified by Fly Fishers International. He enjoys fishing many kinds of water, including saltwater, brackish, streams, rivers, and lakes. He takes his fly tying passion to high levels, with a body of work that consists of realistic art flies and fishable realistic flies.

This realistic stonefly nymph is intended for trout and mahseer (the largest species in the carp family, they can grow up to 9 feet [3 m] long, can weigh as much as 119 pounds [54 kg], and are found in Asian countries such as Indonesia, Malaysia, and Thailand). The level of detail in this fishing fly is incredible. Wirianto's sense of style can be seen by the curvature he builds into the hook shape, which imitates the realistic movement of the swimming nymph.

Catskill-Style Streamers

Tied by Ted Patlen

For most fly fishers, the "Catskill tradition" engenders thoughts of dry flies with stiff tail fibers, thin tapered body, stiff hackle, and upright wings. There is, however, an almost lost tradition of baitfish imitations. In fact, Theodore Gordon (1854–1915), the father of dry fly fishing in America, developed the Bumble Puppy, a suggestive, mostly white streamer about 2 inches (5 cm) long. Herman Christian (1882–1975), who claimed he was the only person Gordon taught to tie flies, developed the slightly larger Candy Cane version.

At the other end of the size spectrum is the Riffle Dace created by Edward Ringwood Hewitt (1866–1957), whose baitfish imitations were intended to be more realistic than the suggestive dry flies used at the time. While the colors, shapes, and sizes found in these early patterns are imitative of natural baitfish, the profiles are suggestive rather than an exact imitation.

These early Catskill streamers were tied by Ted Patlen, a championship-winning fly tyer. He is a traditionalist who tries to use the materials and techniques that were in use during the time that the patterns were developed. For more of his flies, see pages 44, 78–79, and 118.

Darbee Two-Feather Mayfly
Tied by Ted Patlen

Large Catskill-style dry flies originally required large hooks. In the late 1950s, Harry Darbee—a legendary Catskill tyer from Roscoe, New York—developed techniques for using smaller and lighter hooks, allowing for a more delicate presentation that lands the fly with minimal disturbance so as not to frighten wary trout. His technique is seen here in the Darbee Two-Feather Mayfly.

The story goes that Harry's friend Terrell Moore asked him for a fly that would land on the water as delicately as a natural insect. Harry is quoted as saying, "I had been experimenting with an ultralight dressing to imitate our larger mayfly hatches. . . . One night while doubling a hackle for a salmon fly, it occurred to me that perhaps a prepared hackle held the key to what I was looking for." This is Ted Patlen's rendition of Darbee's Two-Feather Mayfly. For more of his flies, see opposite, pages 44, 76–77, and 118.

Early Wet Flies: Scarlet Ibis and Double Parmachene

Tied by Ted Patlen

Dry flies are popular when fish are feeding on natural insects atop the surface. However, 95 percent of the time, fish are feeding below the surface. Early fly fishers knew this and created sunken flies in response.

The all-red Scarlet Ibis (top) was created in Great Britain in the 1700s and found its way to America because of its effectiveness. It is reported to have been artist Winslow Homer's favorite fly. As previously mentioned, horsetail hair was originally used to attach a fly to a line until the gut of the silkworm—a better material for this purpose—replaced horsetail hair. This sample is tied on gut as it would have been in the eighteenth century.

The Double Parmenchene (bottom) is a tandem fly joined by gut. Using two flies allows deeper fishing without adding weight to the line. The Double Parmachene was named for a lake in western Maine (spelled *Parmachenee*) known for its brook trout.

Dry Fly with Inverted Wings

Tied by Pepe Perrone

Some trout are fished over by many fishers and, as a result, see many fly patterns. The more the trout see, the more selective they become. The more selective they become, the more frustrated the fishers become. To fool these "educated" fish requires innovative, realistic flies.

Pepe Perrone of Argentina makes his living as a carpenter, but he has dedicated himself to teaching fly tying and fly fishing since 1985. He was challenged by friends to design a technically difficult fly, and this Dry Fly with Inverted Wings was his answer. It makes use of duck flank feathers tied inverted—pulled in a backward direction—to create a lacy image of the natural insect's wings. It is a delicate technique requiring a light touch and many skills, as a glance at the wings will tell you.

This pattern was designed to be fished for trout in small rivers and streams of northern Patagonia, but Pepe has also used it for carp and pejerrey (*Odontesthes bonariensis*) in the Paraná River, north of Buenos Aires, with much success. Because of its innovation and novelty—no one else is using it—it is effective.

Cicada Indicator Fly

Tied by Steve Potter

Cicadas are insects that emerge every thirteen or seventeen years. How they know whether to wait thirteen or seventeen years is unknown. Their loud call is not made by rubbing their wings or legs together but by the rapid vibration of a pair of membranes called *tymbals* on the sides of their abdomen. Cicadas have been written about since the time of Homer's *Iliad*, and in China some are eaten as a deep-fried delicacy. Steve's Cicada Indicator Fly is not one of the edible varieties.

Steve Potter of Tracy, California—a member of the 2008 team that took first place at the 1st California Delta Bass and Fly Competition—ties this pattern in many sizes to match his needs for fishing in the waters of the Sierra Nevada (these waters supply various species of trout that make a bountiful day of fishing—well worth the time spent at the tying table!) as well as on the California Delta. He began with an old pattern, the Goddard Caddis, and improved it by adding rubber legs and different colors of stacked deer hair so he could see it better in rough water. The use of stacked deer hair makes this fly both colorful and extremely buoyant.

It can be fished alone when cicadas are on the water or as an "indicator" pattern. An indicator is a floating fly to which a sunken fly is attached. When a fish takes the sunken fly, the indicator fly will stop, pause, or twitch, signaling a fish has taken the fly. The take of the sunken fly might be too gentle to be detected without the use of the indicator fly. Fishing the Cicada Indicator Fly with a dropper offers a smorgasbord to entice fish.

For another fly by Steve Potter, see page 82.

Steve's Sculpin

Tied by Steve Potter

Most often, the phrase "matching the hatch" refers to matching natural insects with an imitation, and that's what this fly is. Steve noticed that his hookups increased when his fly matched the color of the local sculpins, which he saw in brown, gray, and black.

Sculpins are small baitfish found on the bottom of water bodies. Their flattened form allows them to live in fast water. Their pectoral fins have an unusual adaptation: smooth on the upper edge and webbed with sharp rays along the lower edge. This modification enables them to grip the bottom, helping them to anchor themselves in fast water. Effective imitations need to be fished along the bottom where trout are accustomed to seeing them.

For another fly by Steve Potter, see page 81.

Seagren's Minnesota Mayfly

Tied by Andrew Seagren

Andrew Seagram wanted to create a nymph that could match huge hatches of burrower mayflies (*Hexagenia*) that are found in his local waters in Minnesota. He developed Seagren's Minnesota Mayfly while trying to figure out how to tie a swimming mayfly that is realistic, has the distinct gills of a mayfly nymph, and is easy enough to tie so that your heart won't shatter if a fish breaks you off. He combined a few techniques from various other patterns, and this fly was the result. The leaflike, feathery gills that extend from the edge of the body make the nymph vulnerable to silting and pollution.

Andrew grew up hunting, fishing, and photographing wildlife in Minnesota. Those hobbies led him to earn a degree and pursue a career in wildlife biology, and fly tying occupies a lot of his time during the winter.

Fox's Mudbug

Tied by Fox Statler

Fox Statler, from Salem, Arizona, has been guiding the North Fork of the White River for over twenty years, and his Fox's Mudbug is an all-time producer for big trout and bass.

Crayfish are high in protein and often abundant. Depending upon the time of the year, they range in size from a fraction of an inch to several inches in length. In the area Fox guides, they can grow up to 10 inches (25 cm) and weigh almost 2 pounds (1 kg).

Fox's Mudbug is tied so the hook point rides up. This is important because Fox prefers to fish it on the bottom among the rocks. His favorite tactic is casting close to the edge of the bank and letting the current slowly pull the Mudbug along the bottom. The metal eyes make have an extra added attraction, as they produce a clicking sound as they bump along rocks. The sound gets the predator's attention even before the fly comes into view. Being forewarned, the predator has time to get ready for an ambush attack.

Royal Coachman Fanwing

Tied by Son Tao

The iconic Royal Coachman Fanwing's colors, peacock green and brown, were designed to catch both fish and fishers. Englishman Tom Bosworth is credited with creating this pattern in the 1830s. An avid angler and coachman for British royalty from King George IV to Queen Victoria, he designed this fly for night fishing. The original design lacked the red silk band, which was added in 1878 by John Haily to reinforce the fragile peacock herl and prevent the fly from unraveling under the teeth of attacking trout.

It was introduced to the United States in the 1890s by Thaddeus Norris, father of American fly fishing and author of *The American Angler's Book* (1864). By 1892, the fly was being sold by the fishing industry giant Charles F. Orvis (1831–1915). Mary Orvis Marbury, his daughter and author of *Favorite Flies and Their History* (1892), when asked what it should be named, said "Oh, that is easy enough; call it the Royal Coachman, it is so finely dressed!" It is a name that continues to be used to this day.

This version, a Royal Coachman Fanwing, was tied by Son Tao, an active-duty Army soldier for sixteen years. Originally from Lancaster County, Pennsylvania, he grew up fishing for trout. For another of his flies, see page 86–87.

Quill Gordon

Tied by Son Tao

This fly pattern deserves special respect in America. The Quill Gordon was one of many ties designed by Theodore Gordon (see also page 76). So important was Gordon's work that he is acknowledged as the father of American dry fly fishing.

Gordon made changes to existing British patterns to incorporate materials that better met the needs of the floating flies used in America's fast-flowing freestone creeks. Two very distinctive materials he used were durable and imitative wood duck flank feathers for wings, and stiff blue dun cock hackles for tails and legs. Once Gordon figured these out, he became the only source for what would later be known as Catskill-style flies. These are characterized by their stiff hackle fiber tail, slender tapered body, stiff wrapped hackle, and upright feather fiber wings.

This tradition became so significant that in 1993, Floyd Franke and Matthew Vinciguerra formed the Catskill Fly Tyers Guild (catskillflytyersguild.org). These men recognized the need for an organization that would preserve, protect, and enhance the Catskill fly tying heritage.

While Son has been fishing for twenty-nine years, he had only been tying flies for ten months when he made this Quill Gordon. For another of his flies, see page 85.

Sugarplum Princess

Tied by Nancy Taylor

Nancy Taylor, a registered Maine guide, chose pink as the primary color for her winning entry, Sugarplum Princess, in a fly tying competition at the Rangeley Region Sports Shop. The competition benefited Casting for Recovery (see more on page 6), which Nancy has been a Recovery Participant Coordinator and Fundraising Coordinator for in Maine for many years. She can be found at fly fishing shows across New England promoting CFR.

Cased Caddis

Tied by Henry Viitanen

There are 14,500 types of caddisflies (order Trichoptera). Their life cycle passes through four stages: egg, larva, pupa, and adult. In the larvae stage they produce silk to make protective cases of gravel, sand, twigs, plant matter, or other debris. They are typically found in running water, and fish species such as brown trout, rainbow trout, and grayling love eating them.

Henry Viitanen's Cased Caddis imitates a case-making caddisfly by using the same kind of fine sand used by the larvae. He is a diverse fly tyer from Finland, and his fly tying styles range from large saltwater and pike flies to small freshwater realistic flies.

He was hooked on the art of fly tying even before he was a fly fisher. He says, "To become skilled, the fly fisher and tyer needs to spend hours behind the vise and also get experience on the water. You must learn the life cycle and habitats of the bug or fish that your fly imitates in order to get the most of your fly fishing experience. You'll appreciate learning as an endless joy and you can always do things better. It is not just catching a fish, and that's why I love fly fishing."

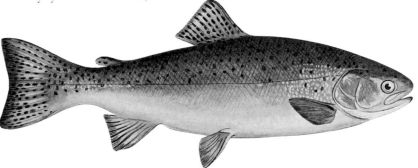

Artfly Mayfly

Tied by Peder "Wiggo" Wigdell

Just as illustration bridges the gap between advertising and fine art, many fly tyers are creating fly patterns that transform utilitarian flies into art pieces. Peder Wigdell from Sweden used a number of materials to create this artful form. The delicate wings, tied Wallywing style, are mallard duck breast feathers. Wallywings, named for the technique's inventor, Wally Lutz, are fashioned from a single bird's body feather. The feather's barbules are pulled back in the opposite direction from their natural position. Next, the barbules on each side are torn away from the central stem and secured to the hook. The remaining central stem is cut off, leaving two wings. The abdomen is clear tubing. The skills required to create such a fly are those of someone who has dedicated many years to the art of fly tying.

This is not meant to be a fishing fly, but an "artfly," something to look at that conjures up dreams of the coming season. You can fish with it if you like, but it won't hold up for more than one or two fish. On the other hand, if it is the fish of a lifetime, it may all be worthwhile.

Peder "Wiggo" Wigdell has tied flies for thirty-eight years. They have mostly been fishing flies, but for the last three to four years he has tied more and more artflies, just for fun. For another of his flies, see opposite page.

One-Feather Fly

Tied by Peder "Wiggo" Wigdell

Sometimes the fly tyer creates a pattern that is so delicate that it gives insight into the mayfly's scientific order name, Ephemeroptera. "Ephemeroptera" is derived from the Greek *ephemera*, meaning "short-lived," and *ptera*, signifying wings. This describes the short lifespan of most adult mayflies, of which there are more than three thousand species.

Wiggo created this fairylike, elegant pattern from red squirrel body hair and one Coq de Leon feather.

When the famous European mayflies hatch in late May and early June (*Ephemera vulgata* and *Ephemera danica*), this is the fly to use. Peder says it is fast and very simple to tie; although not durable, you can easily tie ten of them in less than an hour. Depending on which color the mayfly hatch has in your area, you can change the CDL feather color to better match the hatch. In Sweden, the Medium Pardo (brown) is most useful.

Realism in a Fishing Fly:
King Kray, Killer Cicada, Ultra Brown Stonefly Nymph

Tied by Steve Yewchuck

There's a fine line between realistic fishing flies and show flies not intended to be fished. Many show flies require too many hours and extra-special skills to ever consider getting them wet, let alone risking the chance of losing them to a fish. Realistic fishing flies, however, present just the right amount of primary characteristics of natural insects to fool sport fish. Steve Yewchuck, from Central New York, knows how to build such characteristics into his fly patterns. He is a fly designer for Montana Fly Company and an ambassador for Hatch Outdoors, Korkers, Rising, and Livingston Rod Company.

Steve wanted to tie a realistic-looking Killer Cicada pattern that would sit high and dry all day. The fly, below, is tied with a foam head that pushes water, a Double Barrel™ popper-head abdomen, and a spun deer-hair thorax. The translucent wings add a hint of realism. The fly was designed to fool bass, trout, and any fish that eats big surface bugs.

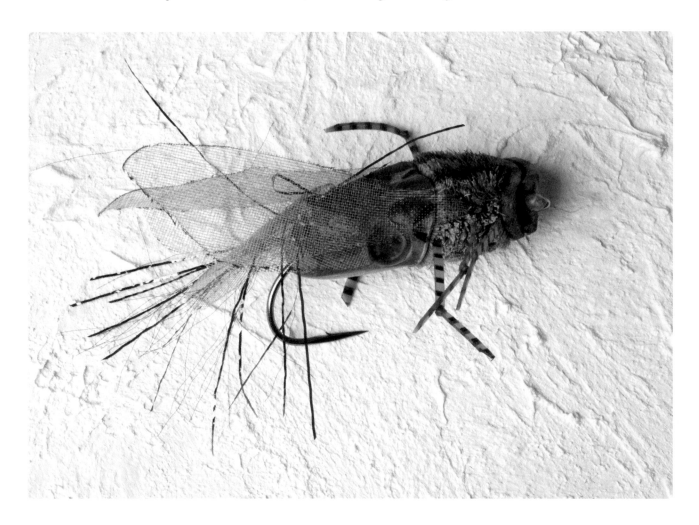

The articulated King Kray (above, top) was designed with two triggers to entice big brown trout to feed. The first trigger is the realistic movement of the marabou tail, which resembles the lifelike action of a fleeing crawfish. The second trigger is the popper-head thorax (a flat-faced fly), which stands up when not in motion and is paired with the movement of the marabou claws that resemble a crayfish in defiance mode. These movements are what make it a deadly brown trout fly.

Some of the biggest trout that Steve has fooled have been on realistic-looking nymphs. In some of the river systems he's fished, nothing would work until he resorted to these flies. One of the important observations he made was that some of the biggest fish preferred nymphs that were oversized compared to the naturals. That's why Steve created his Ultra Brown Stonefly Nymph (above, bottom). For another of his flies, see page 120.

Jungle Cock Stonefly Nymph

Tied by Heinz Zöldi

Heinz Zöldi is from Salzburg, Austria. His Jungle Cock Stonefly nymph (above), with its woven body and a hook bent underneath so that it looks like it's moving, is his favorite pattern. Heinz loves the combination of classic tying materials like jungle cock and modern tying techniques. For him, that's what this nymph is all about: classic meets realistic.

He recalls, "One day, when I was a little boy, I decided to make a fishing lure on my own. I wrapped some wool on a hook. And this was the day I started with fly tying. I wasn't able to fish with a fly rod at this time, but that wasn't important for me, at this moment. I loved to make this kind of lure, and I tried to get better. At first it was hard. I had no vise and no tools, and I had nobody else to train with. But I practiced and practiced and gradually became better. Unfortunately I do not have any flies from this time . . . it would be great to look back and see my progress from the start. So if you start with fly tying, keep your first self-tied flies." For more flies by Heinz Zöldi, see opposite page.

Mayfly with Extended Body and Stonefly Nymph in Motion

Tied by Heinz Zöldi

This mayfly (opposite, top) by Heinz Zöldi has an extended woven body tied over a monofilament base—not an easy task. The Wallywing technique (see page 90) used here is also difficult to learn and requires a gentle touch. The result is a fine, lacy wing with a realistic look.

Heinz's Stonefly Nymph in Motion (opposite, bottom) is one of his favorites because of its spectacular look. When nymphs are swept from the safety of submerged rocks, they twist and turn in an attempt to gain a foothold on rocks before they are intercepted by hungry trout. But, Heinz explains, these are hard to tie. In this fly, the abdomen is made of latex, the legs are cul de canard, and the wing cases are made of Flex-Wing. The head is covered with a jungle cock feather.

When it comes to tying, he says, "I've tied a lot of dry flies, because I fish with dry flies 99 percent of the time. I've also tied a lot of nymph patterns for my father because he prefers nymphs. Then, I did not tie a single fly for a few years because other things, like going out with friends, were more important. One day, I saw a realistic nymph in a magazine and I thought, 'I must tie a fly like this!' I started to tie, and after a few tries, I made my first realistic looking fly. I tried a lot and was never satisfied how the flies turned out and I always try to improve."

SALTWATER FLIES

Saltwater flies are the workhorses of fly fishing patterns, designed to capture fish in the hundreds, if not thousands, of pounds. Tuna, tarpon, sailfish, and even giant marlin are taken on flies of incredible colors. Modern synthetic materials, in colors not found in natural rainbows, stagger the mind when viewed in all their glorious hues.

Claudius Aelianus (see pages 4 and 49) also wrote of fly fishing in saltwater:

> One of the crew sitting at the stern lets down on either side of the ship lines with hooks. On each hook he ties a bait wrapped in wool of Laconian red, and to each hook attaches the feather of a seamew [the common gull].

The depiction suggests that the flies were trolled behind the moving boat.

It wasn't until the mid-nineteenth century that saltwater fly fishing again appeared in print. The British *Encyclopaedia of Rural Sports* (1840) by Delabere P. Blaine depicted fishing in estuaries for a variety of species, however, this angling did not excite fishers of the period and little was written on the subject for the rest of the century.

It took several decades before A. W. Dimock's *The Book of the Tarpon* (1911) began to encourage fly fishing in saltwater. In the United States after World War II, popular writer Joe Brooks's escapades lit a fire under saltwater fly anglers, and species such as bonefish, striped bass, and tarpon were targeted by fly fishers. From that time on, the interest in saltwater fly fishing has grown into a worldwide sport.

Most saltwater fly patterns use synthetic materials because there is a practical limit to the size of fly that can be cast with a fly rod. Synthetics shed water more readily than do natural materials. As a result, large flies can be cast more easily. While most saltwater patterns represent baitfish, the preferred food of big predators, other marine fish foods include shrimp, crabs, and squid. The choice depends entirely on the game fish being targeted. Sharks, while they will eat almost anything, are especially fond of other fish because a large meal satisfies their hunger. They will be tempted by a fly 12 (30 cm) inches long or more. Bonefish and permit, the speedsters of the flats, dine on shrimp and crabs, so a small imitation will get their attention.

Disco Crab

*Tied by **Irhamy Ahmad***

The Disco Crab started as a no-name fly around 2010. Then, upon the insistence of one of Irhamy Ahmad's friends, the fly was christened the Disco Crab Fly (aka the Disco) around 2013.

Irhamy fishes the Maldives on a yearly basis, and his initial goal in creating this fly was to catch the parrotfish that had mesmerized him for years. Hence, the inspiration for the gaudy, disco-inspired colors of the fly. Despite the intention, he has caught all the common tropical species with the Disco—the trevallies, jacks, permit, triggerfish, and bonefish—but not the parrotfish.

The Disco is generally fished slowly in the figure-eight fashion often used for bonefish, permit, triggerfish, and parrotfish, and the take is always at the bottom. In clear flats one may notice that the fish lifts its tail out of the water to grab the fly. This "tailing" behavior tells the angler the fish is feeding.

Irhamy is a Fly Fishers International–certified casting instructor. He started fly fishing in the Walthamstow and Hanningfield Reservoirs in Essex, England in 1986. An avid fly dresser and an occasional bamboo fly rod builder, he travels regularly to fish Indonesia, Thailand, the Maldives, and Mongolia. He is a fly fishing pioneer in Malaysia and has had his own column in a national Malaysian newspaper, *Berita Harian*, since the 1990s. He has also been a bimonthly guest writer for Paul Arden's site Sexyloops for some years.

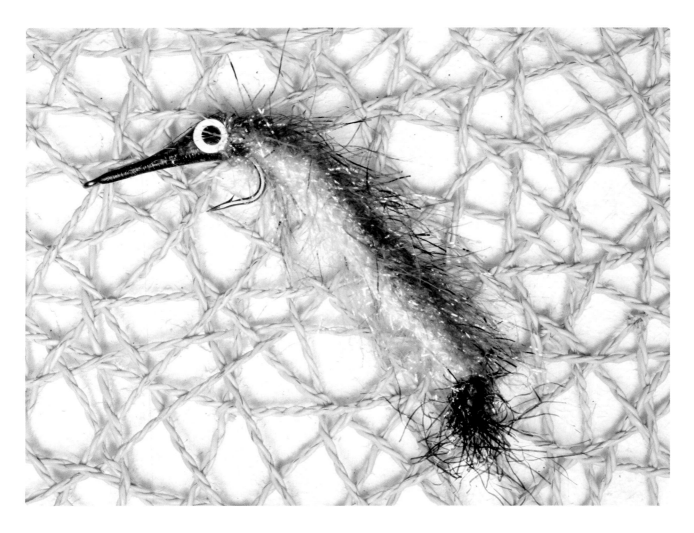

Ezio's Needlefish

Tied by Ezio Celeschi

Needlefish are found around the world, usually in warm, shallow saltwater areas. They vary in length from 1 inch (3 cm) to 38 inches (96 cm). Recently, reports have been coming in that the prominent jaws of even the smallest needlefish are responsible for injuries to fishers.

Ezio Celeschi of Italy needed a bluefish fly to imitate the needlefish in the Mediterranean Sea, because bluefish are fond of them. After some experimentation he developed this pattern. Ezio's Needlefish represents the bill-like jaws by using a long-shanked hook. This design also makes it easier than usual to remove the fly from toothy bluefish while avoiding their sharp teeth.

Ezio's Needlefish is effective when fished close to the banks of incoming rivers, when the estuaries are calm and the needlefish are active. The best time for this fly is on hot summer nights when schools of bluefish are on the feed. Ezio fishes it with alternating slow and fast retrieves on floating lines and uses a steel shock leader to protect the line from the bluefish's row of razor-sharp teeth.

El Diablo Rojo Sardina

Tied by Dennis Gamboa

Dennis Gamboa from British Columbia designed this fly for chasing marlin, roosters, and jack crevalle. The pattern imitates sardine, mullets, and other similar baitfish. Because large flies tend to be difficult to cast, he used lightweight materials with good water-shedding properties. He also selected a unique natural fiber, hair from a domestic breed of sheep found in Europe, the Snow Runner or Nayat. Their translucent hair has very similar properties to that of polar bear, and it has great movement in the water.

Dennis has been tying flies commercially for over twenty years and teaching classes on tying for fifteen. He is known for his original, timeless fly patterns. His business, The Fly Box, produces over thirty thousand flies a year. Dennis has been featured in *BC Outdoors Magazine*. His creativity and design earned him a spot on the Lagartun PRO-Staff team. He is also one of the newest members of the Partridge PRO-Team and part of the Flymen Fishing Company's Commercial Fly Tyer program. For another fly by Dennis Gamboa, see page 102.

Giant Trevally Fly

Tied by Dennis Gamboa

Fish eyes have an abundance of cones. As a result, they are particularly perceptive to differences in colors. Some days their preferences are dialed in to specific preferences. Fly tyers use their skills to create patterns that vary only in terms of color while keeping all other characteristics, sizes, and proportions the same.

The Giant Trevally Fly is used on Christmas Island, an Australian territory. It's quite new and only available from Dennis. Here, it's shown in a variety of colors proven to be effective. The giant trevally is a large member of the jack family, and it can reach weights in excess of 160 pounds (75 kg), so Dennis uses an especially stout hook. For more of his flies, see page 101.

Crab and Shrimp

Crafted by Fred Hannie

Sometimes the biggest saltwater fish dine on the smallest crustaceans, as is the case with striped bass, which take both shrimp and crabs. There are thousands of varieties of shrimp. They range from 0.75 inches to 9 inches (2 to 23 cm) long. They lead a solitary life except for the mating season, so a single shrimp imitation is what striped bass would expect to see. A favorite bass feeding strategy is to pluck crabs from around rocks when the crustaceans get pulled off the rocks in an outgoing tide. When this happens, fly fishers who are prepared can fool the fish. Fred Hannie, from Lake Charles, Louisiana, crafts realistic details into his work to trick fish, as is evident in his crab and shrimp lures. For more flies by Fred Hannie, see pages 65 and 114.

Shrimp

Tied by Konstantin "Kody" Karagyozov

Most tyers develop patterns based on their own needs. This is not one of those times. Most of Kody's fishing is in mountain streams for trout; he does not fish saltwater. He developed his shrimp (above) at the request of other fishers. Based on their feedback, he continued improving the pattern, and now it is a successful fly for many species of saltwater fish.

Kody, who is from Plovdiv, Bulgaria, considers fly tying to be an art form more than as a means of catching fish. His flies are of his own design, and he does not copy the work of other fly tyers. As realistic as many of his flies are, they are intended to be fished. For this reason, Kody builds durability into his patterns. For more of his flies, see pages 66 and 67.

Michaels' Green Portunid Epoxy Crab

Tied by Edward Michaels

Portunid crabs abound in Atlantic waters. Their fifth pair of legs is flattened for swimming, which, along with their strong claws, make them effective predators.

Captain Edward Michaels from Apalachicola, Florida, first tied this pattern (opposite) fifteen years ago exclusively for permit (*Trachinotus falcatus*). He made them most often with a tan carapace and a cream bottom. On a lark he made one in chartreuse and threw it at a permit. It was voraciously gobbled. In time he found that all crab-eaters ate this fly—bonefish, redfish, mutton snappers, and tarpon.

It can be weighted with different amounts of lead, depending on how deep or fast you need it to dive, but it must *never* spin or roll to one side. It *must* track perfectly, even though not stripping it, once a permit sees it, is best.

Squid

Tied by Jimmy Otting

Squid are cephalopods: predatory mollusks with eight arms attached to their head as well as two longer tentacles used for grasping prey. They move by expelling water and some are fast enough to "fly" out of the water for a short distance. They feed on many types of small fish, crabs, and shrimp, and larger squid may feed on smaller animals of their own kind. They are themselves forage fish for many marine sport fish, including striped bass, marlin, tuna, shark, and grouper.

Jimmy Otting grew up in New Jersey and has always fished in fresh and saltwater. His specialty is tying flies for striped bass and false albacore. He's been at it for eighteen years. Whether or not Jimmy enjoys calamari is unknown.

Hollow Beast

Tied by Brian Phelps

The Hollow Beast is one of the many designs by Bob Popovics, who created many of the saltwater flies in use today.

This fly is intended to imitate a menhaden, or bunker. The fly can be 12 inches (30 cm) or longer, but it's intended to be easily cast on a fly rod for use on saltwater fish such as tuna and marlin that measure in hundreds of pounds.

Brian Phelps's Hollow Beast is tied on a monofilament extension with bucktail using the hollow-tie technique. Keeping the collars sparse from the tail to just before the head makes it lightweight and helps it to shed water easily. The last few ties on the hook have more bulk to help give the tail a great natural-looking action when retrieved with a stripping motion.

Brian is a licensed US Coast Guard captain and guide from Long Island, New York. He is also a professional photographer and the owner of Reel Obsession Fishing, Inc.

WARM-WATER FLIES

Modern warm-water fly patterns are the newest to evolve. Bass, pike, muskellunge, sunfish, carp, perch, walleye, and more take these patterns designed to represent baitfish, frogs, mice, and leeches among others. Some fishers use flies as big as those favored by saltwater fishers to catch fish that measure 42 inches (107 cm) or longer. Unusual color combinations and natural materials such as deer hair are commonly used but seldom seen up close. The ingenuity of these patterns will amaze readers.

Though warm-water flies reached the apex of their popularity approximately fifty years ago, they originated much earlier than that, when bass anglers observed the effectiveness of flies for trout and salmon and began to adapt fly patterns to meet their own needs. In 1881, Dr. James A. Henshall, a fishing author and award-winning authority on angling from Ohio, wrote the *Book of the Black Bass—Comprising Its Complete Scientific and Life History Together with a Practical Treatise on Angling and Fly Fishing and a Full Description of Tools, Tackle and Implements.* In its three parts, Henshall covered bass biology, bass tackle, and fishing techniques (including fly fishing).

Henshall wrote in the introduction:

> *This book owes its origin to a long-cherished desire on the part of the author, to give to the Black Bass its proper place among game fishes, and to create among anglers, and the public generally, an interest in a fish that has never been so fully appreciated as its merits deserve, because of the want of suitable tackle for its capture, on the one hand, and a lack of information regarding its habits and economic value on the other.*

Many of these materials—such as feathers, deer body hair, and cork—are still in use today. Deer body hair is hollow and will float for a long time. Contemporary tyers fashion it into amazing shapes for top-water flies. In the late 1880s, artificial, waterproof textile dyes were invented and shortly later, they were used to create colors of deer hair not found in nature. More recently, tyers discovered how to manipulate bundles of colorful deer hair into astonishing color combinations.

In the 1930s, nylon, the first true synthetic material, was invented. More synthetics became available and were pressed into service by tyers. Synthetics are attractive to tyers for several reasons. First, they are available in colors not seen in nature. Second, many have a sheen or sparkle unlike any natural material. Finally, they are inexpensive and easy to work with. Many of the flies in this chapter show how these materials have become common in the fly tyer's art.

Since Henshall's time, virtually every kind of freshwater species has been taken on a fly. Back then, only natural materials were available.

Illustration of bait fishing from the *Book of the Black Bass* by Dr. James A. Henshall, 1881.

Erie Shiner and Silver Pheasant Baitfish

Tied by Kenny Berdine Jr.

Commercial fly tyers tie what works because that's what sells. Kenny Berdine Jr. from Washington, Pennsylvania, knows this well. He owns Fly Tiers Anonymous, a shop that focuses on many species.

The Erie Shiner catches panfish, bass, trout, stripers, crappie, catfish, walleye, steelhead, and pike. How well does it work? In three months Ken sold 1,800 of them. Nothing succeeds like success. The larger Silver Pheasant Baitfish was requested by a bass fisherman who had a general idea of what he wanted. He described his idea, and Ken tried several variations until the fisherman was satisfied. This dedication to detail is how a custom fly tyer develops an enthusiastic following.

Pike Fly

Tied by Corey Cabral

If a fly is to fool a fish, it must have several characteristics: correct size, shape, color, and action. Action means movement in the water that gives the impression of something alive. This is where flies have an advantage over hard lures used by spin fishers and bait casters.

The Pike Fly was created by Corey Cabral, a passionate angler and fly tyer from Ontario, Canada. It's used to imitate baitfish that pike and muskie feed on. The fluid movement of arctic fox, olive buck tail, hackle feathers, and craft fur creates flowing movement in the water that pulses and dances with every bit of current as it moves through the water. The profile it creates is baitfish-shaped.

The mixture of natural and synthetic materials cuts down on the weight of the fly, compared to using just natural materials. The synthetics also allow for water to shed easily, and they impart flash and shiny highlights that imitate the natural look of baitfish.

For more flies by Corey Cabral, see pages 58 and 59.

Press-on Crayfish and Marabou Muddler

Tied by Scott Dooley

Crayfish flies imitate a common food source for trout, bass, pike, carp, and panfish and are excellent flies for rivers, lakes, and ponds where crayfish are abundant. The most distinctive feature on this pattern is the shellback created using press-on nails colored with a Sharpie®.

In white and silver, the Marabou Muddler makes a great imitation of a silvery bait fish. In olive or brown it suggests anything from a leech to a small bottom-dwelling fish. Its pulsating, fish-attracting action comes from a generous wing of marabou, while the bulky deer-hair head makes plenty of subsurface disturbances on the retrieve.

Scott Dooley is from North Algona Wilberforce in northern Ontario, where he fishes mostly for bass on rivers and in lakes. He started fly fishing after inheriting his father-in-law's gear and enormous amounts of fly tying material. Scott learned the basics of tying on YouTube, and then he started tying his own designs.

Bluegill and Turtle

Tied by Fred Hannie

It's not until you see a live specimen side by side with Fred Hannie's lures that you can appreciate the incredible detail Fred captures in his realistic work. His intent in making such accurate imitations is to elicit a second, astonished look from viewers. It's not until the observer picks up one of Fred's creations that one fully understands these creations are not alive. Here are his impressive flies for the wounded bluegill and long-nosed turtle. Both bluegills and turtles are commonly eaten by bass and this fact makes them effective as imitations. For more flies by Fred Hannie, see pages 65 and 103.

Golden Stonefly Nymph

Tied by Aaron Heusinkveld

Aaron Heusinkveld from St. Cloud, Minnesota, was introduced to fly fishing through Project Healing Waters (see more on page 7), and he now fishes mostly for smallmouth bass in the Upper Mississippi River. Aaron's passion of fly tying has grown so much since his introduction to the sport that he's currently working on a mobile fly tying school with the intention of building up the fly fishing community in his area. He volunteers once a week with his Healing Waters chapter and enjoys teaching beginners.

Aaron's Golden Stonefly Nymph developed out of the traditional all-black pattern. Unlike the golden stoneflies that exist in nature, this pattern is entirely gold-colored. As such, it presents itself as an attractor pattern intended to get the fish's attention from a distance.

Bass Flies

Tied by Ed Lash

Ed Lash is a retired orthopedic surgeon living in rural Iowa. He's been fly fishing and fly tying almost fifty years and is now a professional fly tyer specializing in deer-hair flies. His tying revolves around creating bugs that perform as the real ones do in nature. Although he claims not to be an artist, his skills are amazing.

At first glance, it may look like his deer-hair bugs are painted. They are not. Ed accomplishes his creations by tying small bundles of colored deer hair onto a hook shank in a predetermined sequence. When the tying is complete, the body looks like a multicolored porcupine. Next comes shaving the hair to the desired form.

The poppers are good general flies for a variety of species. The minnows are better flies for big fish, and they dive when stripped because they have a diving plane cut into the face. These flies also perform surprisingly well in saltwater inshore too. Although Ed's flies are intended to be fished, they'd also look good in a presentation frame.

Pike Bomb, Pike Bomb Jr., and Pike Snack

Tied by Tim Morales

Pike are among the largest of freshwater game fish. Its genus name, *Esox*, may derive from the Ancient Greek *isox*, meaning "whale-like fish," and it is aptly named. Specimens have been recorded to be 59 inches (150 cm) long and weighing 63 pounds (29 kg). To say they are carnivores is an understatement. While smaller fish are what you would expect to find in a pike's stomach (including smaller pike), ducks, muskrats, and turtles have also been reported. Fly fishers who target these predators need something that will trigger the pike's feeding instincts.

Tim's Pike Bomb (left) and Pike Bomb Jr. (center) were designed for both Michigan pike and muskellunge. The only difference between the two flies is that the Jr. is about 4 inches (10 cm) long, and the full-size Pike Bomb is around 8 inches (20 cm), because you never know what's on a pike's mind.

Tim's Pike Snack (right) is a pattern he created in Denmark with the intention of targeting pike there. It is an articulated pattern with a ton of movement. For more of his flies, see pages 73 and 74.

Early Bass Flies: Cleveland and Holberton

Tied by Ted Patlen

Mary Orvis Marbury, daughter of the fishing-industry leader Charles F. Orvis, realized there was little standardization in fishing flies, so in 1892 she wrote *Favorite Flies and Their Histories* (see page 85). It became a best seller and went through nine printings by 1896. Among the flies included were the Cleveland and the Holberton. In each case, the influence of British full dressed salmon flies is seen: many materials and a multitude of colors.

The Cleveland (top) is a large feather "spoon" wing fly named after a Mr. William D. Cleveland, the "treasurer" of a fishing club that Mary describes as "a jolly club of three, who styled themselves 'the Texas Club'" and who "met in summers to rejoice being together and in fishing 'galore.'" Of interest is the silkworm gut loop at the front of the hook shank. The Holberton (bottom) sports the traditional silkworm gut leader. Wakeman Holberton of New York City designed this bass fly, and Mary standardized its dressing. Ted Patlen, a traditionalist, used the materials and techniques implemented during the time the patterns were developed to create the flies shown here. For more of his work, see pages 44, 76–77, and 78–79.

Form Follows Function: Double Barrel Popper, Lefty's Deceiver (Variation), and Craft Fur Baitfish

Tied by Chris Skinner

"Form follows function" means an object's shape should be based on its intended use. Fly tyers rely on this maxim to effectively attract fish by creating patterns that look like what the fish expect to see.

Chris Skinner is from Garden Ridge, Texas. He taught himself to tie flies primarily for bass. These three flies are built with specific functions in mind. The Double Barrel Popper (bottom), makes a loud popping sound when jerked across the water's surface. The lateral (side) line on all fish is a "hearing" organ that picks up vibrations long before the fish can see their prey. The popping sound alerts the fish that prey is on its way.

The top fly is a variation of a Lefty's Deceiver. Its function is to replicate the colors of a natural prey, and it includes a darker lateral line represented by the black-and-white barred feather. This alignment of colors is consistent with what a bass sees in its food on a daily basis.

The Craft Fur Baitfish (left), is constructed with a round cross section. It is effective because it can be seen from any direction, including above and below. Bass often lie in ambush from below and can be enticed into attacking when this pattern comes into view overhead.

Two-Timing Toad

Tied by Steve Yewchuck

Steve Yewchuck grew up in New York's Catskill region. He loves to add a touch of realism and movement to his creations. He feels movement is a trigger to get big, finicky fish to feed.

Steve designed the Two-Timing Toad for big predator fish like bass, pike, and muskie, which favor a large meal because it yields a bigger payoff in terms of energy gained versus energy expended. Steve's thought about his flies is that he's creating engineered fish food. The ability of a fly to stand up to big-fish attacks is an important consideration for fly tyers. Steve gave this fly durability by running the legs through parachute cord to stiffen them up yet still allow for plenty of movement. For another of his flies, see pages 92–93.

Kurt's Mouse

Tied by Kurt Van Luven

Fish are opportunists. They'll eat whatever comes by. The larger the fish, the larger the amount of fuel required. A mouse represents a hearty meal and will be taken by many varieties of large fish. Predators such as bass and pike often set an ambush from a hidden spot. Those fishers who are specialists, looking for trophy-size fish, can improve their catch by casting to likely ambush areas. That's where Kurt's Mouse shines. It presents a large silhouette when viewed from below, and the movement of surface water as the fly is retrieved gives the fish an early warning that something big, and maybe tasty, is approaching.

Kurt Van Luven from Ontario likes using alpaca fur, because alpacas aren't harmed when their fleece is harvested. It's also easy to dye so you can get any color, and it's very versatile.

Kurt has been a fly tyer for more than a dozen years. He enjoys creating new patterns and variations of traditional patterns.

PART THREE

FLY FISHING SITES AROUND THE WORLD

"If I fished only to capture fish,
my fishing trips would have ended long ago."
—Zane Grey, *Tales of Southern Rivers*, 1924

LOCATION, LOCATION

For those who live the fly fishing lifestyle, the world is little more than a variety of fishing opportunities. Every region has its special attractions, either in freshwater or saltwater. In some places the center of attention is where fresh water meets saltwater. Many prospects are just around the corner and are attainable on foot. Some places are not as trouble-free to get to and require air travel, remote accommodations, and guides to show the way. Here, then, is a sample of what the world has to offer fly fishers and essays on the significance of these opportunities to those who fish with a fly.

Opposite:
Yellowstone, Montana.
Right: Sign on the Beaverkill in Roscoe, New York.

ALASKA

How big are Alaska's fishing possibilities? How about 3,000 rivers, 3 million lakes, and 6,500 miles (10,000 km) of coastline? Today, Alaska's salmon fishery accounts for approximately 80 percent of the North American harvest, but it was almost lost to over-fishing. In 1953, President Eisenhower, a noted fly fisher, made successful efforts to reverse the trend. The state of Alaska enacted legislation limiting sport and commercial fishing bag limits, and the fishery rebounded from disaster.

Alaska's anadromous salmon—the Chinook, coho, and sockeye—are of interest to fly fishers, and hundreds of fishing lodges and outfitters cater to anglers who want to catch these types. The major Alaskan trout species targeted by fly fishers include the rainbow, Dolly Varden, and steelhead. Regardless of the species, Alaska's wilderness vistas entice as many fishers as the fish do.

Above: A rainbow trout, caught in the Kvichak river, Alaska. **Opposite:** Angling in Alaska; many remote destinations are only reachable via plane.

"The charm of fishing is that it is the pursuit of what is elusive but attainable, a perpetual series of occasions for hope."

—John Buchan

Opposite: Fly fishing for salmon amid brilliant fall foliage on the Ninilchik River, on Alaska's Kenai Peninsula. **Above:** Spawning salmon in Ketchikan Creek, Alaska.
Following pages: Salmon fishing on the Chilkat River delta outside of Haines, Alaska.

THE AMAZON RIVER

South America's Amazon River discharges the world's largest volume of water, equal to twelve Mississippi Rivers. The Amazon starts in Peru's Andes Mountains, less than 100 miles (160 km) as the crow flies from the ocean, but its sinuous course stretches its length to more than 4,000 miles (6,500 km) making it the longest river in the world. With over 1,000 tributaries, the fishing possibilities are virtually infinite.

Sport fishing began in the Amazon in the early 1990s. The 3-foot (1-m) long giant peacock bass is among the most-targeted Amazon species. Named for its bright hues, the giant peacock bass is among the most aggressive, aerobatic, and hard-fighting fish on Earth. Occasionally found in the 50-pound (25-kg) range, they require stout equipment. Leave your 4- and 5-weight trout rods home; giant peacock bass need 8-, 9-, or 10-weight rods, reels, and lines.

Giant peacock bass are not the only species fly fishers go after. Others include alligator gar, a prehistoric-looking fish, which can grow to ten feet and 300 pounds (135 kg); pirarucu (or arapaima), the second-largest freshwater fish in the world, which can grow to nearly 17 feet (5 m) and 450 pounds (200 kg); and carnivorous piranhas of horror-movie fame, which offer a change of pace.

Numerous outfitters offer a variety of fishing accommodations. After flying in, one can stay in luxury lodges, riverside cabins, floating cabins (river levels vary by season), or cabin "trains" that are floated from location to location, depending on conditions.

Opposite: The ferocious teeth of a piranha, photographed in the state of Amazonas, Brazil. **Right:** An angler proudly displays a giant peacock bass caught in Brazil's Amazon River Basin. **Following pages:** Fishing for peacock bass on the Uatumã river, a northern tributary of the Amazon.

BATTENKILL RIVER

The 59-mile- (95-km-) long Battenkill River is a tributary of the Hudson River. This nationally known river rises in East Dorset, Vermont, and continues into New York, meeting the Hudson River in Easton, New York.

The Battenkill is known for its trout fishing and especially for its wary and difficult brown trout and abundant brook trout. Deep pools, large rocks, overhanging banks, and large streamside trees provide protection for the fish population. Spring seeps keep the water cool throughout the year.

Not too long ago, the river was in trouble. A decline in fish populations was experienced in the 1990s, and a 2005 study determined the decline in fish size and population was due to loss of protective habitat due to floods and misuse of land adjacent to the river. The Batten Kill Watershed Alliance was formed and, along with its partners, began creating new shelters, which demonstrated that replacing habitat features previously lost could increase trout populations.

The best dry fly fishing on the Battenkill is from mid-May to mid-July, when numerous mayfly hatches appear. In summer months the "rubber hatch" (people floating on the river in rubber tubes) take over the river and cause some consternation for diehard fly fishers.

Rapids and large rocks on the Battenkill River.

Early summer is the ideal time for dry fly fishing on the Battenkill.

Above: Angling on the Battenkill; **left:** Fly fishing in front of the iconic Arlington Green Covered Bridge, built across the Battenkill in 1852 in Arlington, Vermont.

My Zen

Bruce Curtis

I remember the first time I started to fly fish and to photograph the sport. I'm an action photographer used to shooting football and basketball for Sports Illustrated—hardly a serene occupation. In contrast, it was so quiet on the river, and the people I encountered fly fishing were so nice to me, giving me tips on how to fish and how to capture the whip in casting.

One day I was photographing on the Battenkill River in Vermont, and a man walked up to me and asked what I was doing. I replied that I was working on a book on antique fly fishing equipment with the American Museum of Fly Fishing—and lo and behold, the stranger was actor Kurt Russell. We had a great time talking and fishing together.

Anglers always tell me about the one that got away. I parry with my story about being on a photo shoot with Jacques Cousteau to photograph the great white sharks off the Great Barrier Reef in Australia. When I tell them I went into the shark cage and a 15-foot (4.5-m) great white shark hit the cage, they are fascinated. That was the fish that didn't get away.

I will always be photographing projects, but I don't know if I like photographing fishing or just like to fish, but I get a warm feeling either way. This is such a beautiful and quiet sport—it is my Zen experience.

"It is certainly a greater pleasure to outwit the game by a clever imitation of a fly. . . . But the essential charm, we think, lies beyond the mere use of a fly. . . . The gentle but continuous activity of fly fishing gives it interest; the endeavour to put the fly accurately and delicately just where the angler would have it, makes it as absorbing as any trial of marksmanship."

—Leroy Milton Yale, "Getting out the Fly Books," *Angling*, 1896

This page and opposite:
More scenes of trout fishing
on the Battenkill.

BEAVER CREEK, COLORADO

Beaver Creek begins its journey from near the top of Pikes Peak in Colorado. It is known for its wilderness setting, and access is difficult for all those unwilling to hike into steep canyons without trails. In contrast to the upper river area is the section below the Skaguay Reservoir where it becomes a gentle meadow creek. As a result, this is the most frequently visited area with the greatest fishing pressure. Brook, brown, and rainbow trout are all found in this watershed.

Opposite: A fly fisherman precariously perched on a rock in the middle of Beaver Creek, in Colorado.
Above and right: Anglers plying the waters in more peaceful areas of Beaver Creek. **Following pages:** A bucolic bend of Beaver Creek.

*"Angling may be said to be so like the mathematics,
that it can never be fully learnt."*

—Izaak Walton, *The Compleat Angler*, 1655

This page: Beaver Creek fly fishing.
Opposite: Colorado's Skaguay Reservoir,
which also boasts an ample supply of trout.

BEAVERKILL RIVER

The Beaverkill, a tributary of the East Branch of the Delaware River in New York's southern Catskill Mountains, is cloaked in fly fishing legend. The continuing purity of its fertile water attracts fly fishers from around the world. They come to experience world-class dry fly trout fishing supported by generous, predictable mayfly hatches. Many famous pools and runs are known by name to those who wade its water, and although most of the river above Roscoe is privately held, the balance, from Roscoe to its junction with the East Brach of the Delaware River, is open to all fishers.

So celebrated is the Beaverkill that it is considered the birthplace of American fly fishing, where American fly fishing pioneers such as Theodore Gordon and John Burroughs felt quite at home. In the early 1800s, because of its proximity to New York City and the quality of its fly fishing, it became the first fishing resort destination in the

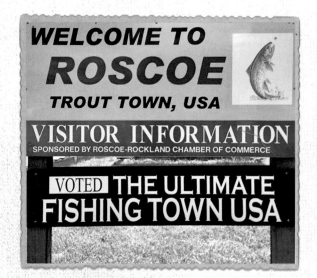

Opposite and this page: Fly fishing on the celebrated Beaverkill in the Catskills, along with a sign welcoming fishers to Roscoe.

United States and supported several fishing lodges and resorts. At that time, fishers would stay for extended periods to enjoy the celebrated fishing.

In the 1850s, the Beaverkill's brook trout fishery was in decline, initiating one of the earliest conservation movements in America. This led to the creation of conservation watchdogs that have overseen this 44-mile (71-km) stretch of river to this day. In the 1950s, conservationists rallied again to fight against the plan to divert the river to ease construction of Route 17. This, too, was

successful, and in several places Route 17's roadway is elevated above the river's unaltered riverbed.

In 1979, Joan and Lee Wulff opened the Wulff School of Fly Fishing, which is still active today on the Beaverkill just upstream of the Beaverkill Valley Inn. That inn is just one of the many motels, bed-and-breakfasts, and other lodging options available today, and reservations for May and June, the peak fishing months, need to be made nearly a year in advance.

> *"To many great fly fishers, the Beaverkill is the standard by which all other trout streams are judged. It is the first and the oldest in reputation."*
>
> —Ed Van Put, *The Beaverkill: The History of a River and its People*, 1996

Opposite and this page: Serene moments on the Beaverkill.

The Beaverkill Valley Inn and Fly Fishing Center

Discover a Last Great Retreat to Fly Fishing

This inn sits quietly alongside the legendary Beaverkill River, known by fly fishers as the birthplace of American dry fly fishing. Its watershed embraces thousands of acres of undeveloped land and clear mountain streams. This region of New York's Catskill Mountains is two hours from Manhattan, yet its wilderness experience is a lifetime away.

More than one hundred tributaries flow into the Beaverkill along its 45-mile (70-km) journey to the Delaware River. The Beaverkill Valley Inn is set on 60 acres (25 ha) within Catskill Park, close to the upper Beaverkill, which flows down from the headwaters peaks almost 4,000 feet (1,200 m) high through preserved wild forests and conserved meadows. On this land, visitors enjoy 1 mile (1.6 km) of private fly fishing.

American fly fishing pioneers such as Theodore Gordon and John Burroughs felt at home in the Beaverkill, which remains a source of legend and wonder. In 1979, Joan and Lee Wulff opened the Wulff School of Fly Fishing, which is still active today on the Beaverkill just upstream of the inn.

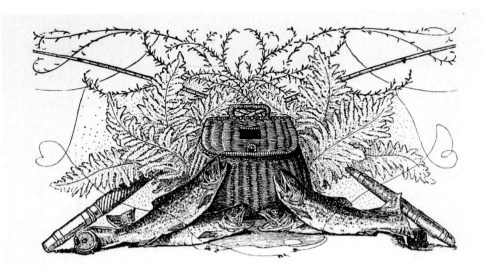

Above: Four fly fishers in position on the Beaverkill; **right**: Fly fisherman checking rocks to find out what insects have hatched. **Following pages**: More Beaverkill views.

BOCA GRANDE, FLORIDA

Boca Grande is on Gasparilla Island off the western coast of Florida, 100 miles (160 km) south of Tampa on the Gulf of Mexico. The Calusa tribe, native inhabitants of the area since c. 5000 BCE, originally settled Gasparilla Island around 800 CE. British settlers are reported to have harpooned tarpon in the 1700s. The first mention of a rod and reel catch was in 1885. With the completion of a railway in the early 1900s, anglers from around the world could reach the island. Today, more than five thousand tarpon are landed in a typical eighty-day tarpon season, making Boca Grande the tarpon capital of the world.

Above: A tarpon, or "silver king," jumping out of the water; Boca Grande is known internationally as the world's tarpon capital.
Opposite: Fly fishing off a boat in the warm waters off Boca Grande.

CANADA

Canada has Atlantic salmon fly fishing on the east coast, Pacific salmon fly fishing on the west coast, and every imaginable type of fly fishing in between.

The star of eastern Canadian fly fishing is the Atlantic salmon. Rivers such as the Miramichi, Bonaventure, Grand Cascapédia, and Restigouche are among the most famous, and they continue to be destinations for serious fly fishers—many of whom continue using variations of traditional full-dressed salmon flies.

Moving west, brook trout, lake trout, smallmouth bass, and walleye add to the varieties of game fish available to the fly angler not only in rivers, but lakes as well. Many outfitters offer wilderness experiences, some of which can only be reached by floatplane.

In the middle provinces, northern pike and muskies make their appearance and test the skills of fly anglers requiring heavy tackle and large flies. Great Slave Lake and Great Bear Lake boast lake trout that weigh up to 70 pounds (32km).

To the far west, principal attractions include five varieties of Pacific salmon, Arctic char, and steelhead. The Thompson, Skeena, Copper, and Yukon rivers entice fly anglers with their reputations for large Pacific salmon and steelhead.

Fly fisherman at dawn in Nova Scotia.

Above: Fly fishing near Yellowknife, the capital of the Northwest Territories.
Opposite: A fly fisherman on the Pinware River, in Labrador, holds on tight as a salmon on his line jumps into the air.

"*River angling certainly requires more delicacy and art in its pursuit, but that of the Lakes of Canada has a character of expansion and sublimity which must also recommend it to the reflecting mind.*"

—William Agar Adamson,
Salmon-Fishing in Canada, 1860

A majestic view of the Rockies in Alberta.

> *"No better waters were ever known,*
> *Where fly is cast or troll is thrown."*
>
> —*Fishing Resorts Along the*
> *Canadian Pacific Railway*, 1887

Above: A woman fly fishing for salmon on the Margaree River on Cape Breton Island, Nova Scotia. **Opposite**: Freshwater fishing in crystal clear turquoise waters, British Columbia.

MADAGASCAR

Madagascar, off the southeast coast of Africa, is the fourth-largest island in the world. Its freshwater system is one of the most unusual on the planet. Many of its species are "living fossils" and belong to the most primitive of species. According to the World Wildlife Fund, "The freshwater fishes of Madagascar are considered the island's most endangered vertebrates. Habitat degradation, siltation, temperature increases due to deforestation, agriculture, overfishing, and the introduction of exotic species are considered the main causes of native species decline."

The majority of fly fishers target the plentiful varieties of saltwater fish, such as grouper. However, they may be missing the thrill of Madagascar's tigerfish. The tigerfish is vicious like a piranha but is a lone predatory hunter. With two rows of wolflike fangs, it is the fish of nightmares. Another "interesting" fact is that the tigerfish has rudimentary lungs and can navigate across land for short distances. Pleasant dreams.

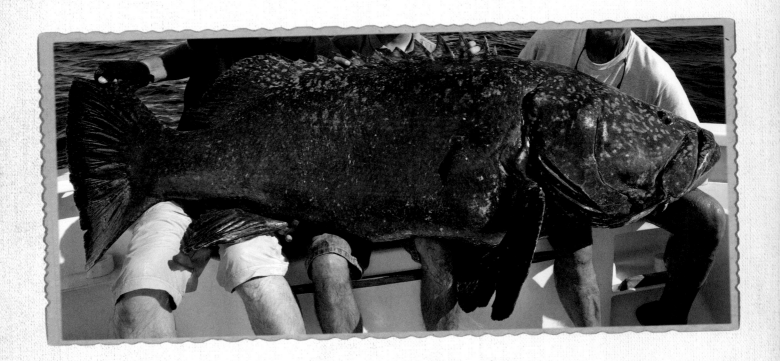

Above: A giant grouper caught off the coast of Madagascar.
Opposite: A view of Nosy Iranja, a small key off Madagascar known as the Island of Turtles; the waters around this area are teeming with kingfish, grouper, marlin, and more.

MONTANA

It would take a lifetime to fish every trout stream in Montana. This is not only Big Sky Country, it's "big trout country" as well.

Many of Montana's rivers have been designated as Blue Ribbon trout streams, meaning that the water quality and quantity can sustain a fishery; the public has ample access to the river; natural reproduction can occur without the need for artificial stocking; and the river is able to endure high fishing pressure. Special regulations, such as creel and size limits, are in force to protect these government-designated Blue Ribbon waters.

There are several important Montana rivers for fly fishing. The Smith River is so popular that in a recent year 8,000 people applied for just 1,175 permits to float it. The Boulder River, a tributary of the Yellowstone River, stays cool in summer months and is a classic mountain river with plenty of pocket water to protect fish. The Firehole River is in Yellowstone National Park and sees plenty of fishing pressure. Early season is best because the river warms during summer months and the fish become inactive. In 1958, a landslide created Quake Lake. Its outflow, the Madison River, is shallow, allowing for fishing in pocket water. The Bighorn River is considered to be the best river in the state because of its trout populations and year-round fishing opportunities. The Blackfoot River was featured in Norman Maclean's book *A River Runs through It and Other Stories* (1976); the film adaptation directed by Robert Redford (1992) introduced thousands of fly fishers to the wonders of western fly fishing.

Opposite and above: Fly fishing in the pristine waters of the Blackfoot River in Montana. **Right:** Rainbow trout caught and released in Montana.

"[Fly fishing] taught me many, many things about grace. I think it's one of the most graceful things an individual can do out in the woods."

—Norman Maclean, interview with Nicholas O'Connell

Left: Cutthroat trout caught and released in Montana; **Below**: Fly fisherman in a Montana river. **Opposite**: Fly fishing in the Yellowstone. **Following pages**: Sunset fishing on Montana's Blackfoot River.

MONTAUK, NEW YORK

Montauk, on eastern Long Island, is 118 miles (190 km) from Midtown Manhattan but light-years away in terms of fishing opportunities. Striped bass, false albacore, tuna, sharks, and bluefish are among the stars in this location, with hundreds of fishing charter boats plying the waters.

Of particular interest is the striped bass. In early autumn, the bass journey southward, passing Montauk in one of the largest wildlife migrations on Earth. At this time, every seaworthy craft is loaded with anglers as they leave port in search of *Morone saxatilis*.

Shark fishing has also long been a staple for anglers departing Montauk. A variety of sharks are found within 20–30 miles (30–50 km). Thresher, mako, blue, and, of course, great white sharks are all found near Montauk.

As an added bonus, in 2016, a great white shark nursery was discovered just a few miles off Montauk. Great whites can live for 70 years, grow to 25 feet (7.5 m) and weight 5,000 pounds (2,300 kg). For the faint of heart, there is also some freshwater pond fishing nearby.

Above: Surf fishing off Montauk. **Opposite**: More surf fisherman, near the historic Montauk Point Light lighthouse, first lit in 1797 (top); a great white, one of the species of sharks to be found off the Montauk coast.

PECOS RIVER, NEW MEXICO

The Pecos River starts its journey at a 12,000-foot (3,700-m) elevation on the eastern slope of the Sangre de Cristo Mountains in New Mexico and runs through Texas. Nearly 1,000 miles (1,600 km) later, it joins the Rio Grande. The first 20 miles (30 km) are designated a Wild and Scenic River by the United States government.

The section inside the New Mexico National Historical Park is of special interest. A pilot program that began in 2017 mandates that three 1-mile (1.6-km) sections are restricted to only three anglers each per day from September 14 to October 6. This restriction provides access to the otherwise closed section of the park, ensuring a pristine environment and a true wilderness experience.

Left: Rainbow trout caught and released in the Pecos River.
Opposite: A bend of the Pecos River, where introduced brown trout and rainbow trout can be caught with typical trout stream patterns.

Crazy for Fly Fishing

Bill Buchan

I found my grandfather's fly rod in the attic when I was eight years old. I took it to a stream and then to the lake. My dad didn't fly fish, but he did take me fishing, so I probably put a worm on the end of the line. That was the start of my love for fishing.

Next was tying flies and learning to read the river. I looked under logs, stones, in the water and cobwebs, and under bridges to learn the hatch. This made fly fishing interesting, to see what the fish were feeding on and to learn how to match the stages in the insect's life from nymph to adult and, most importantly, catch fish.

I lived on my sailboat in the late 1960s thru the 1980s in Nantucket, and I would take my dingy out and fly fish for stripers and bluefish. Onlookers would make fun of me and stare at me like I was crazy. They were correct—I am crazy for fly fishing. I travel far to fish and love the unguided venture that is part of the challenge and the solitude that nature offers.

By the way, I'm off to my favorite stream to fish.

Bill Buchan of Stowe, Vermont, is a respected fisherman in the Northeast of the United States and writes many articles about the sport. He also is a world-class sailor, and, with his very large sailboat, he has sailed around the world fly fishing.

PORT CHARLOTTE, FLORIDA

Fly fishers are excited about the fact that Port Charlotte's harbor is Florida's second largest tidal estuary. Not only is this harbor more than 700 square miles (1,800 square km), it has nearly 200 miles of saltwater canals and nearly 200 miles (320 km) of freshwater canals. As a result, the fly fishing is excellent on the saltwater flats as well as in the backcountry brackish water.

The mixing of saltwater from the Gulf of Mexico and freshwater rivers makes the estuary home to cobia, grouper, tarpon, redfish, and barracuda. There are so many tarpon that numerous tarpon tournaments are held in the estuary each year. Tarpon fishers are smiling because this area held the record (216) for most giant tarpon caught in a single year.

Sight fishing, fishing to catch fish that are seen cruising nearby, is a favorite tactic on the flats and among the mangroves. Sight fishing makes this kind of angling similar to hunting because it is necessary to spot the quarry before it spots you and disappears into deeper water.

Opposite: Punta Gorda wetlands near Port Charlotte. **Above:** Fly fishing off Port Charlotte.

RUSSIA

There are two outstanding areas in Russia that are home to unbelievable fishing. The Kamchatka Peninsula is at the eastern extreme of Russia, adjacent to both the Bering Sea and the Pacific Ocean. The Kola Peninsula is adjacent to Norway at Russia's far western border. These areas became destination fisheries in the early 1990s, and their continued attractiveness for fly fishers is testament to their quality.

Kamchatka's rivers, such as the Elovka, Kapushka, Medved, and the Shishey, boast rainbow trout up to 35 inches (90 cm) that take dry flies all day long. This is unusual because trout seldom feed on top of the water for extended periods of time and trout of this size seldom eat flies, preferring a mouthful of baitfish. The area is so remote that poachers are unable to reach it and fishers require a helicopter to get there.

The Kola Peninsula, lying almost entirely above the Arctic Circle, is among the elite Atlantic salmon fisheries in the world. Here, salmon rivers are numerous and the outsize salmon are among the most difficult to land on a fly. The rivers here include the Litza, Umba, Yokanga, Varzuga, Kharlovka, Rynda, and Ponoi. Early expeditions to this remote peninsula experienced logistical problems such as shortage of aviation fuel and insufficient food for visiting fishers. This left many fishers questioning the worth of facing such fiascos regardless of the fishing quality. Despite the risks, demand for access to this fishery grew, and all logistical problems have long been resolved.

Opposite: Fly fishing in one of the rivers on the Kamchatka Peninsula in northeast Russia. **Above:** Spawning sockeye salmon in a river in Kamchatka.

"It is impossible to grow weary of a sport that is never the same on any two days of the year."

—Theodore Gordon

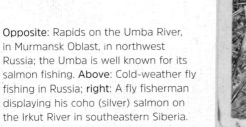

Opposite: Rapids on the Umba River, in Murmansk Oblast, in northwest Russia; the Umba is well known for its salmon fishing. **Above:** Cold-weather fly fishing in Russia; **right:** A fly fisherman displaying his coho (silver) salmon on the Irkut River in southeastern Siberia.

SAN JUAN RIVER, NEW MEXICO

This major tributary of the Colorado River has been the traditional border between the Navajos' land to the south and the Utes' land to the north. At nearly 400 miles (640 km) in length, it starts as snowmelt in the San Juan Mountains and flows to the Colorado River at Glen Canyon.

The San Juan's reputation as a world-class trout fishery was built on the stretch starting below the dam on New Mexico's Navajo Lake. This is a tailwater fishery, meaning the river is drawn out of the lake from 40 feet (12 m) or more below the lake's surface. As a result, the water temperatures remain a constant 45 degrees Fahrenheit (7°C) year-round. Trout can be fished when summer air temperatures are in the 90s (30s Celsius) or in the winter when the air temperature is below freezing.

This river is the home and namesake of the fly pattern the San Juan Worm. Literally nothing more than a 2-inch (5-cm) length of chenille tied to a hook, the San Juan Worm's reputation is known worldwide.

This page and opposite: Fly fishing on the San Juan River in New Mexico.

The Majesty of Fly Fishing

Sue Anne King

Fly fishing is my personal journey into an enchanted spectacle of nature that opens up a flow of energy at its source. It is transformative to be secluded, fly fishing in the brisk running waters of a river or creek far away from the daily routines of urban life that dull the senses. To catch a trout is like a miracle full of mastery and perfection.

Getting to the point of being properly geared up and traveling to an unknown destination takes days of preparation. My fly fishing adventures grew out of a fascination with location photography that captures the beauty of nature.

The fly fishing equipment and artful array of flies are overwhelming. Having a career as a fashion editor, the look of a fly fisher inspires me. Earthy colors, short utility vests with multiple pockets, easy button-down shirts, substantial lace-up boots, fun hats, fingerless gloves, and overall waders! The part of dressing up comes naturally; however, help was needed when learning how to cast. After some lessons and practicing in the driveway, I was on my way to the next step: tying knots and attaching a fly to the line. My partner, an expert in the details, guided me through the learning curve. The excitement built, and I was ready to experience the San Juan River in Farmington, New Mexico.

Navajo State Park is a world-class fly fishing destination. The San Juan River is surrounded by a southwestern landscape displaying brilliant colors and vast mesas. My senses heightened as I carefully ventured out into the river and made my first cast. The sounds of nature, cool currents flowing across my waders, air fresh with the earth's scent created a poetic reality. The movement of a fluid cast and anticipation of catching a trout thrilled me. Being encompassed by something greater than the sport is the awesome gift of the Earth's wonder, and its serene, majestic presence offers my spirit a deeply felt peace.

Fly fishing is a high point in my life. Catching a trout is an adventure that takes skill. Whether hiking into a canyon in Colorado to find the perfect stream or taking a chance at

Beaver Creek, the day is always mixed with pleasure and challenge. A graceful cast dances across the stream in wait for the trout that will feed on the chosen fly that lands perfectly on the water's surface. Fly fishing quiets the mind and heart while enlivening a spiritual sense of being in touch with the universe. With a little luck, all those elements come together and a beautiful rainbow trout is caught and released.

Sue Anne King, a world-class fly fisher, has traveled around the world fishing in extreme places and writing articles about her travels.

SCOTLAND

Richard Franck, a British army captain and author, was the first to write about fly fishing in Scotland, in his book *Northern Memoirs* (written in 1658; published in 1694). In the early to mid-nineteenth century, fly fishing became trendy and British fishers went off to Scotland, Ireland, and Norway.

As discussed previously, during this time full dressed Atlantic salmon flies were being developed. The gaudy flies, often requiring 30 different materials, were easy to obtain because the British Empire spread around the world and provided colorful feathers with which to make the flies.

There are nearly seventy-five Atlantic salmon rivers in Scotland, and hosted fishing trips are a major commercial activity. Some rivers, such as the Spey, Dee, and Tay continue to enjoy almost mystic reverence. However, Atlantic salmon fishing is not the only attraction. Trout fishing for freshwater species is abundant. Sea-run varieties are also taken at the mouth of rivers. An early form of lake, or lough, fishing involves drifting a boat with the wind and dapping flies so they dance on the surface. This continues to work well for those experienced in this type of fly fishing.

Opposite: Fly fishers on the River Spey near the village of Craigellachie in northeast Scotland, during the opening of salmon season in 2014.
Above: Landing a salmon on the River Tweed, which flows along the border between Scotland and England.

*"He that catches fish, and fisher too,
Has done as much as man or art can do.
Honour's the bait for one; but silly flies
Are mortal engines for the scaly fries."*

—Richard Franck, *Northern Memoirs*, 1694

Above and right: Casting on the River Spey. **Opposite**: Salmon and trout fishing in a loch on the Shetland Islands, Scotland (top); a wild brown trout caught in the loch (bottom).

STUART, FLORIDA

Stuart is located on Florida's southern Atlantic coast. This area is also known as Florida's Treasure Coast because it is the site of many Spanish galleon shipwrecks. Although many of the sunken treasures have been found, the fishing continues to attract tourists to this area.

Species available close to shore include ladyfish, pompano, permit, redfish, snapper, sea trout, sheepshead, and snook. Farther offshore, species include blackfin tuna, cobia, barracuda, blacktip shark, bonito, wahoo, dolphin, jack crevalle, sailfish, tarpon, and Spanish mackerel. Sailfish, though, are the big attraction in Stuart. So big, in fact, that Stuart is known as the sailfish capital of the world. Sailfish are billfish with dorsal fins spanning almost the entire length of their back. For the most part, sailfish keep their dorsal fin flat against their body while swimming. Only when the sailfish attacks its prey does it raise the fin. Underwater videos show how several sailfish hunt together, surrounding a school of baitfish and raising their dorsal fins like curtains to help corral the baitfish into a dense ball just before they attack.

Top: A sailfish gracefully leaping; **Above:** Aerial view of the coast of Stuart, Florida, the sailfish capital of the world. **Opposite:** Father and son fly fishing at sunset in the waters off Stuart.

TAOS, NEW MEXICO

Taos is in north-central New Mexico in the Sangre de Cristo Mountains. It was not incorporated until 1934. A relatively small population of approximately six thousand means there is little pressure on the area's trout fishing.

Several rivers in the Taos area are popular for trout fishing. The Rio Grande, 20 miles (32 km) southwest of Taos, boasts brown trout up to 20 inches (50 cm). The Rio Hondo, 10 miles (16 km) north of Taos, has a faster gradient than the Rio Grande, and trout find protection is the deeper, slower pools. The Rio Chiquito (aka Little Rio Grande) is a small river with small, skittish trout. The Rio Pueblo is a larger stream in a rugged canyon and demands care when moving along it.

Fly fisherman on the Rio Grande, New Mexico, in autumn.

June Morning in the Berkshires

Michael D. Coe

Some very effective fishing flies are so small that their beauty can only be appreciated with a hand lens. But these catch trout, too!

It is a beautiful morning in June. I am alone, knee-deep in a river in the Berkshires of Massachusetts, at the bottom of a gorge. The dawn sun has just begun to light the tops of the surrounding hills, but the pool I am standing in is still deep in shadows. Along the river margins sandpipers hunt for food, and I can hear the plaintive song of a nearby wood thrush. From time to time I can see the bright side of a trout beneath the rushing water as it turns to mouth an insect nymph from the river bottom, but there is little activity on the surface. Suddenly, twenty feet in front of me, there is a tiny splash, no more than a wink of light, and I make a quick cast to a point just above it. The fly on the end of my long leader is a Griffith's Gnat, a tiny concoction of peacock and chicken feathers not much bigger than a fleck of dust, attached to my leader by a tippet as fine as a spider's thread. To a surface-feeding fish, it would look like a midge—a major trout food.

The fly floats over the spot where that rising fish must be watching, and I keep my eyes on it. Splash! The loose line races through my fingers as the hooked, and by now panicked, trout races off down the pool. A few minutes more and he lies in my net as I gently remove the fly from the corner of his mouth and free him into the stream.

Michael D. Coe is one of the foremost Mayanist scholars and a professor emeritus of anthropology, Yale University. Sport fishing has been his passion since the age of six, and it has taken him to six of the world's seven continents. It is said that when Steven Spielberg was making the movie Raiders of the Lost Ark, *Coe was the inspiration for Indiana Jones.*

WEST CORNWALL, CONNECTICUT

The Housatonic River rises in Vermont and runs through Massachusetts before entering Connecticut. The stretch in West Cornwall is among the best trout fishing water in the state. The 10-mile (16-km) special Trout Management Area, overseen by the state, begins above the famous covered bridge in West Cornwall and continues downstream. Creel limits and minimum-size limits protect this fishery. What draws fly fishers to this wilderness-like haven in densely populated Connecticut are the abundant 12- to 18-inch (30- to 46-cm) holdover trout that survived the winter.

This page, opposite, and following pages: Trout fishing—and trout caught—on the Housatonic in West Cornwall, Connecticut.

YELLOWSTONE RIVER

The 700-mile (1,125-km) Yellowstone River is a tributary of the Missouri River. It rises in Wyoming's Younts Peak in the Absaroka Range at the 12,800-foot (3,900-m) elevation, runs through Montana, and descends to 1,800 feet (550 m) in North Dakota. It is the largest free-flowing river (dam-free) in the United States. Its tributaries are too numerous to mention, but the headwaters of each are home to naturally reproducing fish such as rainbow, cutthroat, brook, and brown trout.

Because the Yellowstone River is so wide, many fishers prefer to hire a guide and float the river, casting to likely trout holding areas. Guided float trips can last from one to several days, depending on the angler's preference.

Fishing interest peaks in late May through early July, depending on elevation, when the salmonfly (*Pteronarcys californica*) makes its appearance. These large stoneflies love fast, rocky water typically found in gorges. They grow up to 3 inches (7.6 cm) long, and their emergence arouses a feeding frenzy in even the largest trout in the river as the fish gorge themselves on the bounty of hatching salmonflies. There is also a downside to this hatch. Once the trout have stuffed themselves, they may not feed again for several days, leaving the fly fishers shaking their heads in spite of the numerous salmonflies still showing on the water. However, there is a solution. The salmonfly hatch begins at lower river elevations and, over several weeks, moves steadily upstream. Once the fish are satiated, moving several miles upstream to where the hatch is just beginning can expose hungry trout that are just beginning to find salmonflies hatching.

Opposite: A fly fisherman's stunning view on the Yellowstone River in Wyoming; **above:** a fly fisher in Montana displays a giant salmonfly.

Left, bottom, and opposite: Bucolic scenes on the Yellowstone; below: Rainbow trout caught and released on the Yellowstone.

Tying, Fishing, and Learning

David Klausmeyer

In the very early 1970s, a department store in Tulsa, Oklahoma, sponsored a weekly television show dedicated to hunting and fishing. I was about twelve years old, and I never missed an episode. Since this was the northeast corner of the Sooner State, the fishing centered on black bass, crappie, and catfish, the species of greatest interest to local anglers. I suppose there was an occasional episode dedicated to trout, but those fish lived in only a couple of rivers flowing from large reservoir dams. The hunting episodes featured quail, deer, turkey, and pheasant.

One warm Wednesday evening, this program showcased a gentleman who was casting to bass with a fly rod. He fished small farm ponds using a canoe, a watercraft almost as rare as a fly rod in Oklahoma. This fellow slowly paddled his canoe using his left arm, and he held his fly rod with his right hand. What I remember most is that it all made perfect sense to me: the canoe, the rod, and the flies. And he was catching fish!

At the end of the half-hour show, the host announced that this gentleman would be in the sporting goods section of that department store the following Saturday to tie flies and talk about fishing. I asked my parents to take me to see him.

I spent that Saturday morning watching him make bass bugs that looked like small field mice. He'd wrap a hook with thread and then tie small clumps of deer hair to the shank. The hair flared when he tightened the thread. After adding several bunches of hair to the hook, he secured and snipped the thread. Next, he trimmed the small ball of fuzzy deer hair into the shape of a mouse; he even added a leather mouselike tail to the fly. Once again, it all made perfect sense to me. I didn't own a fly rod, and this was the first person I had ever met who even knew how to fly fish, but it didn't matter; I had to learn how to make my own flies.

Like most fledgling fly tyers, I started with a fly tying kit that contained a haphazard collection of poor-quality materials that would challenge the talent of even the most experienced tyer. I struggled and eventually made a few flies that looked like misshapen

hummingbirds. Somewhere along the line I acquired my first fly rod, and I struggled to learn how to cast. I had no teacher, but my local library had a few fly fishing and tying books. I read, practiced my tying and casting, and with time I caught a few fish.

That was more than forty years ago, and I am still tying, fishing, and learning. But as much as I love to tie and fish— and I've enjoyed a bit of success with both—I'm still trying to recapture the sense of wonder I felt watching that gentleman make his small imitations of field mice, and the joy I experienced catching my first fish with one of my own flies.

David Klausmeyer has written many books on fishing flies and is editor-in-chief of Fly Tyer magazine. He is one of the most respected authors in the business and has won many awards for his writing.

ACKNOWLEDGMENTS

Fly fishing appears to have been discovered independently in several locations around the world. It is fitting, then, that the contributing fly tyers, whose work appears here, should also represent an international flavor.

Some of the participating fly tyers are professional tyers working in high-volume commercial operations. Several others specialize in developing new patterns never before imagined. Others are fishing guides who work hard to find fish for their clients. A few are fishers who enjoy fly tying as a means to survive winter days when fishing is not possible. Regardless, of their ilk, there would be no book without their involvement and willingness to share what has taken many of them years to discover.

President Jimmy Carter has written the foreword to many books. I believe this is the first fly fishing and tying book to enjoy his written commentary. Most fly fishers know the President and Mrs. Carter are lifelong fly fishers who have fished around the world. It was an unparalleled thrill to learn that President Carter would write the foreword for this book. Many thanks, Mr. President.

New York's Catskill region is the birthplace of dry fly fishing in America. It is fitting that it is also home to the Catskill Fly Fishing Center & Museum, in Livingston Manor. This organization's raison d'être is to preserve and share the fly fishing tradition and spirit of the fly fishing community. Glenn Pontier, Executive Director, provided us with information about, and access to, the organization's facility, vision, and programs. It is clear that the CFFCM's reputation as the largest such organization in the world is richly deserved.

Several individuals offered essays that grace these pages. Thanks to Michael D. Coe, a world-class sportsman and noted Mayan scholar who took time from his busy schedule to share his passion for fly fishing in the observations and photos he provided and his enthusiasm for the book. Bill Buchan wrote about fly fishing based on his far-ranging travels on *Stiletto*, his eighty-foot sailboat. Sue Anne King eloquently described her love of the sport and shared images from her travels in New Mexico and Colorado. Thanks also to Thomas J. Gilligan, who all those decades ago displayed the great art of casting.

Several contemporary fly tyers shared their patience, ingenuity and artistry in perfecting their craft. Sue Post, owner of the Fur, Fin & Feather Sport Shop in Livingston Manor, New York, toured me through a great selection of specialty fly fishing gear and demonstrated her skill at fly tying. Lee Weil demonstrated her talents while presenting a daylong tutorial at the CFFCM. Paul McCain, owner of River Bay Outfitters, one of Long Island's top fly fishing outfitters, enthusiastically shared his knowledge and images from Montana. Paul introduced his son, Owen, a talented fly tyer who kindly showed his skills on several occasions.

Richard Chianella patiently edited photos in Photoshop. Victoria Ward shared her treasure trove of art materials. Lorraine Gilligan provided a critical eye to photographic compositions.

A book is only an idea until a publishing house brings it to life. The specific skills of talented individuals must come together unerringly if the idea is to be revealed as envisioned. The folks at Sterling Publishing created the vehicle to carry our initial idea forward. Our thanks to the following professionals at Sterling Publications: Barbara Berger, executive editor, for her encouragement and support in pursuing the concept and presentation of this project; Gavin Motnyk, interior designer, for the beautiful design; Igor Satanovsky, cover designer, for the stunning cover; Christopher Bain, director of photography, for his invaluable assistance and additional photography; Hannah Reich, project editor, managing editorial; Lorie Pagnozzi, interior art director; Elizabeth Mihaltse, cover art director; Jo Obarowski-Burger, creative director, and Fred Pagan, production manager. Let's do it again real soon.

Tony Lolli
Bruce Curtis

GLOSSARY

A

Abdomen: The belly section of an insect.

Action: The movement of a fly in the water.

Anadromous: Migratory fish such as salmon and steelhead that live in the ocean but migrate up freshwater rivers to spawn.

Atlantic salmon (*Salmo salar*): The "king of gamefish," noted for its leaping ability when hooked. The record fish, caught in a net off Scotland in 1960, weighed 109 pounds (50 kg), which is much heavier than the average weight which ranges from 8 to 12 pounds (3.5 to 5.5 kg). The Atlantic salmon differs from Pacific salmon in that it does not die after spawning and can return to the ocean and run its home river again to spawn. Genetically, it is the same as the smaller landlocked salmon that were cut off from the ocean during the last ice age.

Attractor: A fly pattern that does not imitate any organic organism but is designed to invite fish to eat it.

B

Baitfish: Small fish eaten by larger predatory fish.

Bamboo: See *Cane*.

Barb: The rear-facing spur near the hook point designed to prevent the hook from coming loose.

Bass bug: A fly for catching warm-water species such as bass. They are constructed from hollow deer-tail hair to float for extended times.

Beadhead: A type of fly constructed with a metal bead at the head to give extra weight to the fly so it will sink quickly.

Beard: Material tied under the fly body and extending to the point of the hook, making for a fuller profile.

Bluefish (*Pomatomus saltatrix*): A marine pelagic (living in the open ocean) fish found in temperate and subtropical waters. It is prized for its fighting ability.

Bluegill (*Lepomis macrochirus*): A variety of sunfish fed upon by bass and other warm-water predatory fish.

Bobbin: A tool used in fly tying to hold the tying thread.

Bodkin: A fly tying tool, resembling a needle with a handle, designed to pick out stray materials and apply head cement.

Bonefish (*Albula vulpes*): A wary marine fish prized for its speed when hooked.

Brook trout (*Salvelinus fontinalis*): A type of Arctic char distinguished by pink spots surrounded by pale blue halos.

Brown trout (*Salmo trutta*): A member of the trout family distinguished by a brown background with dark brown-black spots.

Bucktail: The hair from and species of deer often used to make a long wing on flies.

C

Caddisfly: A common and important aquatic insect that resembles a moth in its flying, adult stage. In its underwater stages, some build a case of sand and some use small sticks. As the insect grows, it adds materials and makes its case larger.

Cane: The preferred name for the bamboo used in making fly rods. A round length of cane is split into strips that are planed to desired dimensions in order to make a five-sided rod.

Casting for Recovery (CFR): A nonprofit organization supporting breast-cancer survivors through fly fishing.

Catskill Fly Tyers Guild: An organization dedicated to preserving, protecting and enhancing the Catskill fly tying heritage.

Catskill-style flies: Flies originating in the Catskill Mountains of New York and of a specific form and requiring specific fly tying techniques. Held in high regard because the Catskill area is the home of dry fly fishing in America.

Char (*genus Salvelinus*): A fish related to the trout family and that prefers cold water. Brook trout and lake trout are examples.

Cheek: Usually found in salmon flies, it is a short feather just behind the eye.

Cicada: A large insect up to 2 inches (5 cm) long with clear wings. Well-known types include the thirteen- and seventeen-year cicadas.

Claudius Aelianus: A Roman who was the first to write about fly fishing in c. 200 CE.

Collar: A circle of feather or fur ahead of the body and behind the eye of a fly.

Crab: A common marine crustacean eaten by many marine fish.

Craft fur: A long-fiber synthetic material valued for its ability to shed water.

Crayfish: A small lobsterlike crustacean found in rivers and lakes.

Cul de canard (CDC): French for "butt of the duck." These fine-fibered feathers come from the oil gland and are prized for their floating ability.

D

Darbee, Elsie and Harry: Legendary Catskill fly tyers.

De Santis, Valter and Ennio: Designers of the Facocchi style of dry fly.

Dead drift: The most desired drift of a fly, occurring when the fly floats with the current, as does a natural insect, without being pulled in any direction.

Deceiver: A style of fly with long feathers that was originally designed by Lefty Kreh, American fly fishing legend.

Dette, Mary and Walt: Legendary Catskill fly tyers.

Disc drag: A mechanical device on contemporary fly reels that tightens as a fish attempts to pull line from the fly reel.

Double taper: A fly line profile which is tapered at both ends and has a middle section of thicker-diameter line.

Dragonfly: A large aquatic insect found in ponds. At rest, it holds its wings at 90 degrees to its body.

Dropper: A submerged fly attached to a floating fly.

Dry fly: An insect imitation designed to float on the water.

Dubbing: Material, most often natural fur, twisted around tying thread to create a noodle that is wound around the fly shank to make a body.

E

Emerger: An insect imitation created to represent the stage between a subsurface swimming nymph and a winged adult.

Epoxy: (Usually) a two-part adhesive coating which hardens delicate tying materials so a predator fish's teeth cannot destroy the fly.

F

Fan-wing: A style of dry fly wing made of two body feathers arranged so they stand over the body of the fly like an umbrella.

Ferrule: A device for joining two sections of a rod.

Flash: Any one of several synthetic materials designed to reflect light and get the attention of fish.

Flat wing: Usually a baitfish-imitation wing with two feathers tied flat over the body.

Floatant: A waterproofing liquid or paste used to prolong the floating ability of dry flies.

Fly Fishers International (FFI): A community of fishers and conservationists formally known as the International Federation of Fly Fishers

Fly line: A light woven cable of Dacron covered by a floating layer of plastic. It is designed to be cast by the rod, taking the fly along with it.

Fly reel: A spooled device used to hold fly line.

Fly rod: A type of fishing rod designed specifically to cast a fly line.

Full dressed: A term for salmon flies constructed of many colorful materials, and were originally designed in the eighteenth and nineteenth century.

G

Gaspé Peninsula: A Quebecois Canadian territory well known for its Atlantic salmon fishing.

Giant trevally (*Caranx ignobilis*): A warm-water marine game fish that can reach 160 pounds (75 kg).

Gordon, Theodore: The father of American dry fly fishing.

Gut: In the eighteen hundreds, leaders were made of the gut of silkworms because of its strength.

H

Hackle: A feather, usually from a rooster, often used to form a tail on a streamer fly.

Hackle pliers: A fly tying tool used to grip feathers as they are wound around the hook shank.

Hair wing: A baitfish-imitation wing using hair rather than feathers.

Hatch: When subsurface forms of aquatic insects emerge from the water and fly away as adults.

Hook: The steel object upon which a fly is tied. Hooks are manufactured in many shapes and sizes.

I

Indicator: The name given to a floating fly when a dropper fly is attached below. Also, a small float for fishing a weighted nymph deep.

Intruder: A large saltwater fly with two hooks connected by monofilament or a steel leader. Long hackle is tied on the leading hook and covers the trailing hook, thereby reducing the weight of the fly.

J

Jassid: A small, terrestrial insect often imitated by using a jungle cock eye nail (from the neck of the jungle cock) as a flat wing.

Jungle cock: A feather from the neck of the Indian jungle cock. It often appears as eyes on full dressed salmon flies.

L

Larva: The immature crawling and swimming stage of an aquatic insect.

Lateral line: A "hearing" organ that all fish have that picks up vibrations.

Leader: The clear monofilament section between the fly line and the fly. The thick end is attached to the fly line and the fly is attached to the thin, tippet section.

Limerick: An Irish town known for its fishing and hook-making industry.

M

Marabou: The light, fluffy feathers from the African marabou stork or wild turkeys. Once used for feather boas, today they are prized for their ability to wave seductively in the gentlest of currents.

Marbury, Mary Orvis: The daughter of the fishing industry giant Charles Orvis and author of *Favorite Flies and Their Histories*, the first volume of standardized fly patterns.

Marlin: A leaping marine fish in the Istiophoridae family valued for its size. It can reach nearly 1,000 pounds (450 kg).

Matching the hatch: Matching the appearance of natural insects with a lookalike imitation.

Mayfly: A common freshwater insect of importance to fly fishers because of its widespread presence as a trout food.

Monofilament: A clear line made from nylon that is also occasionally used as a fly tying thread.

Mudbug: Another name for crayfish.

Muddler: A style of baitfish imitation that usually has a head made from spun deer hair.

Muskellunge (*Esox masquinongy*): Also known as "musky," this is the largest member of the pike family. In the Ojibwe language it means "ugly pike."

N

Needlefish: A long, thin warm-water marine fish in the Belonidae family favored by larger predator fish.

Nymph: The immature stage, between crawling larva and winged adult, of any aquatic insect.

P

Pacific salmon (genus *Oncorhynchus*): There are five types of Pacific salmon: Chinook (also known as the "king," species name *tshawytscha*), coho (also known a "silver," species name *kisutch*), pink (*gorbuscha*), sockeye (*nerka*), and chum (*keta*). The first two are of primary interest to fly fishers, with the Chinook attaining a record weight of 83 pounds (38 kg). Pacific salmon hatch in freshwater rivers, go to the sea to mature, return to the river of their birth to spawn, and die after spawning.

Palmer: The technique of wrapping a feather around the hook shank or body to create the look of bulk without adding weight to a fly.

Parachute: A dry fly style of hackle wound around the wing rather than the hook shank.

Pattern: The "recipe" or list of materials specified for making a particular fly.

Peacock herl: The metallic green fibers from a peacock tail feather.

Permit (*Trachinotus falcatus* and *T. goodei*): An extremely elusive marine fish prized for its fighting ability.

Pike (*Esox lucius*): An elongated warm-water predatory fish.

Popper: A fly designed to maximize water disturbance when jerked along the surface of the water.

Project Healing Waters (PHW): A national nonprofit organization dedicated to helping disabled military veterans through fly fishing.

Pupa: A sedentary form of an aquatic insect that is between the larva and adult. In land insects, it is the cocoon stage.

Q

Quill: The long, thin section pulled from the stem of a feather. It is most often used to wrap a segmented-looking body around the hook shank.

R

Rainbow trout (*Oncorhynchus mykiss*): A member of the trout family distinguished by a longitudinal band of red color on its sides.

Reel seat: That part of a fly reel used to attach the reel to the fly rod. It is usually made of threaded or sliding metal bands.

Retrieve: The act of pulling the fly back after a cast has been made.

Rubber hackle: Rubber strands that easily move in the water and are used for legs on flies.

S

Salmon fly: Multicolored, brilliantly hued flies for Atlantic salmon.

Sardine: A small, abundant marine baitfish that is a member of the herring family and is frequently eaten by many larger predatory fish.

Sculpin: A flat-bodied, bottom-dwelling freshwater baitfish in the Cottidae family.

Scud: A small, freshwater, shrimplike crustacean.

Sea-run: A term describing fish that are spawned in freshwater, migrate to the ocean to mature, and return to freshwater to spawn.

Shank: The long part of a fishhook to which materials are tied to create a fishing fly.

Shrimp: A small, abundant marine crustacean favored by marine game fish.

Smallmouth (*Micropterus dolomieu*): A variety of warm-water bass.

Spawn: The mating act of fish reproduction.

Spey flies: A style of salmon flies with long, flowing hackles. They were originally created for salmon on the River Spey in Scotland.

Spinner: The mating form of a mayfly that appears in great numbers and then falls dead on the water after its eggs are laid.

Spool: The round moving part of a fly reel that holds the fly line.

Squid: A cephalopod with eight arms and two tentacles that are used for grasping.

Steelhead (*Oncorhynchus mykiss*): A migratory rainbow trout that lives in the ocean but ascends freshwater rivers to spawn.

Stonefly: Flat-bodied, dull-colored aquatic insects eaten by many game fish.

Streamer: A hair-wing or feather-wing fly imitative of a baitfish.

Striped bass (*Morone saxatilis*): These fish are found along the North American Atlantic coast. Commonly in the 8–40 pound (3.5–18 kg) range, the record is 124 pounds (56 kg). Because they are anadromous, some have been successfully stocked in freshwater lakes, where they reproduce.

Synthetic Living Fiber (SLF): A glistening fiber used to increase the reflective quality of flies.

T

Tag: Most often found on full dressed salmon flies, it is a narrow band of reflective material found at the rearmost end of the fly body.

Tapered leader: A fly leader made of monofilament constructed with a thick butt end that narrows to a thin tippet to which the fly is attached.

Tarpon (*Megalops atlanticus*): A marine fish often reaching 200 pounds (90 kg) and favored for its leaping ability and speed.

Tenkara: A traditional Japanese fly fishing method that uses a rod with the line tied to the tip but no reel.

Terrestrial: Land- rather than water-based insects often taken for food by fish.

Thorax: The section of a fly that is ahead of the abdomen where the legs are attached.

Throat: See *Beard*.

Tip section: The narrowest segment of a fly rod.

Tippet: The thin end of a fly leader to which the fly is knotted.

Trico: Short for the genus *Tricorythodes*, a tiny but abundant fly that is an important food for trout.

Trigger: An element, such as eyes, built into a fly to entice a fish into striking the fly.

Tube fly: Any fly pattern tied on a hollow tube through which the leader runs before a hook is attached.

U

Underwing: Most often found in full dressed salmon patterns and streamers, the underwing lays along the body and is topped with another wing of different color.

UV resin: A type of liquid cement that turns solid after it is treated with ultraviolet light. Its purpose is to hold materials in place and make the fly durable.

V

Variant: A dry fly with oversized hackle and often no wings.

Vise: A mechanical device used to hold a hook during fly tying.

W

Wallywing: The technique invented by Wally Lutz in which a dry fly wing is created by grooming a feather's fibers back in the opposite direction from which they naturally lie and tying them down. This makes for the appearance of a lacy mayfly wing.

Wet fly: An insect imitation designed to be fished under the surface. They can be constructed to imitate insects or baitfish.

Whip finish: A fly tying knot used to prevent the tying thread from coming loose when the fly is being fished.

Z

Zonker: A style of baitfish imitation that uses a strip of rabbit hide with the fur attached. When retrieved, the soft rabbit fur ripples, giving the impression of a live creature.

CONTRIBUTORS

Irhamy Ahmad of Malaysia is a Fly Fishers International–certified casting instructor. He travels regularly to fish Indonesia, Thailand, Maldives, and Mongolia. You can find him at www.facebook.com/irhamy.ahmad.

Mike Algar runs Freestone Fly Fishers Ltd., a fly fishing outfitter in Calgary, Alberta. You can find him at www.facebook.com/FreestoneFlyFishers.

Pål Andersen is a competitive fly fisher who has won many competitions, both individually and on teams. You can see his work on flyfishnorway.com.

Jerry Atencio lives in New Mexico. His work can be seen on Instagram under the name *droptine909* and on the YouTube channel Team A10CO.

Walter "Wolly" Bayer is a self-taught tyer who travels Europe teaching how to tie facocchi's flies. You can visit his website, Outlaw Fly Fisher, at outlawflyfisher.com and find him at www.facebook.com/OutlawFlyfisher.

Kenny Berdine Jr. from Washington, Pennsylvania, owns the shop Fly Tiers Anonymous. You can visit the shop online at www.flytiersanonymous.com and www.facebook.com/flytiersanonymousshop.

Andrew Bogley of Hunker, Pennsylvania, is a self-taught and dedicated fly fisherman. He is also a fly tyer, writer, and amateur aquatic entomologist.

Bill Buchan of Stowe, Vermont, is a respected fisherman in the northeastern United States and writes many articles about the sport. He also is a world-class sailor, and, with his very large sailboat, he has sailed around the world fly fishing.

Corey Cabral from southwestern Ontario, Canada, is a professional fly tyer who works with the Canadian online retailer and wholesaler Frosty Fly. You can see his work under the name *fanaticaltyer* on Instagram and at www.facebook.com/corey.anthony.7503.

Ezio Celeschi of Italy has his work posted on www.facebook.com/ezio.celeschi.

Jonathan Charlton of Saskatoon, Saskatchewan, has been tying for only five years but is already an accomplished tyer. His work can be seen at on Instagram under the name *chuckinbugs*.

Michael D. Coe graduated from Harvard College in 1950. He then worked for the CIA as a case officer in Taiwan. He later returned to Harvard and received his PhD in anthropology. He is considered one of the foremost Mayanist scholars of the late twentieth century and is a professor emeritus of anthropology at Yale University.

Sport fishing has been his passion since the age of six. Inheriting his grandfather's fly rod eventually led him to fly fishing, a sport which has taken him to six of the world's seven continents, from the Russian Artic to Patagonia, from Australia's "Top End" to the Amazon, from the Bahamas to Christmas Island. While doing field archaeology, Coe always tried to pick ancient sites near rivers, lakes, or shorelines where good fishing was said to be guaranteed (and usually was). It is said that when Steven Spielberg was making the movie *Raiders of the Lost Ark*, Coe was the inspiration for Indiana Jones.

Mark H. V. Corps's work can be seen at www.facebook.com/mark.h.corps.

Bruce Corwin from Boca Raton, Florida, ties both show and fishing flies. Bruce's flies have been featured in several books, and he was profiled in the spring 2016 issue of *FlyTyer Magazine*. Bruce's webpage, A Fly Fisher's Art, can be found at brucecorwin.com, and you can visit him at www.facebook.com/A-Fly-Fishers-Art-187515664402.

Scott Dooley from Algona Wilberforce County in northern Ontario has his work posted on the Facebook group Dooley & Ernest Fly Tying, which can be found at www.facebook.com/groups/1828673487404939.

Jan Edman of Sweden has been a guest fly tyer at the Catskill Fly Fishing Center & Museum, and his work can be seen online at www.facebook.com/Jan-Edman-Fly-Tyer-478272282341546.

Fabrizio Gajardoni of Rimini, Italy, is a master at the tying vise. He has won several medals at fly tying competitions, and you can see his work on his website, Gaja Flies, at gajaflies.it. He has contributed to the Italian magazine *Sedge & Mayfly* as well as the famous American *Art of Angling Journal*.

Daniel Galhardo of Colorado is the founder of Tenkara USA. You can visit the company online at tenkarausa.com and learn more about this style of fly fishing through Daniel's book, *Tenkara*, which can be found at www.tenkarabook.com.

Dennis Gamboa of British Columbia is the owner of commercial fly business The Fly Box. He has been featured in *BC Outdoors Magazine* and is a contributing writer for the website Inspired Spaces (inspiredspaces.net). Dennis is known for his original, timeless fly patterns. You can visit the store fishingflybox.com and www.facebook.com/pg/TheFlyBoxx.

Fred Hannie of Lake Charles, Louisiana, is well known for his realistic lures. To find out where you can meet Fred, see his current work, and learn about his techniques, visit him at www.realisticflytying.net and www.facebook.com/RealisticFlyTyerFredHannie, where you'll see damselflies, bluegills, crabs, a soft-shell turtle, frogs, toads, potato bugs, beetles, crickets, honeybees, grasshoppers, katydids, carpenter ants, wasps, and spiders.

Aaron Heusinkveld of St. Cloud, Minnesota, was introduced to fly fishing through Project Healing Waters, and he continues to volunteer at his local chapter. He also teaches fly tying around his community. More of Aaron's work and teaching activities can be seen on Instagram under the name *alltiedupflytyingschool* and on his website, All Tied Up Fly Tying School, at alltiedupflytying.wixsite.com/flytyingschool. His step-by-step video teaching how to tie the Golden Stonefly Nymph pattern, and others, can be viewed at www.youtube.com/channel/UCfWuQSHU53_G7kCUTORT4_Q.

Konstantin "Kody" Karagyozov from Plovdiv, Bulgaria, ties all kinds of flies from patterns of his own design. You can see his work on his website, Kody Flies at kodyflies.com, and at www.facebook.com/kodysflies.

Martin Langlands of South Island, New Zealand, owns Troutlands Guide Service and has been a professional fly tyer since the early 1980s. His work can be seen on the Troutlands website, troutlands.com, and at www.facebook.com/troutlands.

Ed Lash of Iowa creates amazingly detailed flies. His work can be seen at www.facebook.com/ps22bassbugs. He also has a YouTube channel called Ps 22 Bass Bugs, found at www.youtube.com/channel/UCVlO2kKEniJ-slaPXh2IJYA, where you can see videos of Ed doing his magic.

Larry Leight, from North Carolina, is a modern tyer who is committed to preserving the tradition of feather-wing streamers. His work can be viewed on Streamers 365, an on-line blog, The Streamers List by Chris DelPlato, and on two Facebook pages: The Classic Wet Fly and Streamer and Larry Leight.

Bill Litz of Rexford, New York, has been an avid fisher since middle school. You can find him on Facebook under the name Fish Flymaker at www.facebook.com/profile.php?id=100015509809342

Paul Martin lives in Auburn, Maine, and can be found online at www.facebook.com/profile.php?id=100000202387375.

Dave Matenaer from Wisconsin has been tying flies for twenty-two years. David shares his fly tying on Facebook group pages The Art of Fly Tying & Fishing and The Fly Tying Community.

Owen McCain is a competitive fly tyer from Baldwin, New York.

Christof Menz is the founder of the Pro-Guides Flyfishing Company in Austria. His work can be seen on his website, Pro-Guides Flyfishing (pro-guides.com), and at www.facebook.com/ProGuides.

Edward Michaels of Apalachicola, Florida, can be found at www.facebook.com/edward.michaels.524.

Tim Morales of Michigan is a relatively new fly tyer. His work posted on the Facebook groups Fly Tying Adventures and Coldwater Fly Tying as well as on Instagram under the name coldwater.fly.tying.

Edward "Muzzy" Muzeroll is an avid tyer who lives in Sidney, Maine, and can be found online at www.facebook.com/black.argus.

Wirianto Ng is a fly casting instructor in Indonesia and is certified by Fly Fishers International. He fishes around the world, and his work can be seen on Instagram under the name wirianto_ng and on Facebook's The Fly Fishing Group at www.facebook.com/groups/506771179445716.

Jimmy Otting has been tying flies for eighteen years, specializing in flies for striped bass and false albacore. You can see his work at www.facebook.com/Hooks-by-rollcast-486478454789987.

Ted Patlen is the winner of seven world flying tying championships. He can be found online at streamers365.com/ted-patlen and www.facebook.com/ted.patlen.

Pepe Perrone of Argentina has taught fly tying and fly fishing since 1985. His website is Pepe Flycast, pepeflycast.com.

Brian Phelps is a licensed United States Coast Guard captain and guide from Long Island, New York. He is also a professional photographer and the owner of Reel Obsession Fishing, which you can find at www.reelobsessionfishing.com.

Sue Post is a long-time fly tyer and co-owner of Fur, Fin & Feather Sport Shop in Livingston Manor, New York. You can find her store online at www.facebook.com/pages/Fur-Fin-Feather-Sport-Shop/133504640122778.

Steve Potter of Tracy, California, was a member of the 2008 team that took first place at the 1st California Delta Bass and Fly Competition. You can see his work at www.facebook.com/steve.potter.39982.

Justin Sanders is a professional fly tyer from Vancouver, British Columbia. You can find his website at flytyingforcescustomtiedflies.com, and his Instagram name is *ftfcustomtiedflies*.

Andrew Seagren of Minnesota has his work on Instagram under *aseagren19* and at www.facebook.com/andrew.seagren.

Chris Skinner of Garden Ridge, Texas, has his work posted to Facebook under *Christopher Skinner* at www.facebook.com/FishinFool713/photos?pnref=lhc.

Fox Statler has been a guide on the North Fork of the White River in Arizona for over twenty years.

Barry Stokes of Victoria, British Columbia, can be found online at www.facebook.com/barry.stokes.77 and his work can be seen on Partridge Pacific Northwest's Facebook page, www.facebook.com/partridgepacificnorthwest.

Sun Tao, an active-duty Army soldier from Lancaster County, Pennsylvania, has his work on several Facebook group pages: Fly Tying Patterns and Videos, Fly Tying With Uncle Cheech, Fly Tiers Anonymous, Fly Tying Community, and The Fly Fishing Community.

Nancy Taylor is a registered Maine guide and a Recovery Participant Coordinator and Fundraising Coordinator for Casting for Recovery. She can be found online at www.facebook.com/profile.php?id=100013708365302.

Kurt Van Luven of Ontario has been tying flies for over twelve years and sells custom flies as well as bucktail and marabou jigs. His work can be seen at www.facebook.com/kurtsflyshop.

Henry Viitanen is a fly fisher and tyer from Scandinavia. His tying styles range from large saltwater and pike flies to small freshwater realistic flies. His work can be seen on Instagram under the name *instanrii*.

Lee Weil is a professional fly tyer who designs and sells ties, teaches classes on the art of tying, and competes in tying contests around the world. You can find her online at www.leeweilflies.com and www.facebook.com/Lee-Weil-Custom-Tied-Flies-388039961376447.

Peder "Wiggo" Wigdell of Sweden has been tying flies for almost forty years. You can see his work at www.facebook.com/wiggoflytying.

Steve Yewchuck of central New York is a fly designer for Montana Fly Company and an ambassador for Hatch Outdoors, Korkers, Rising, and Livingston Rod Company. He has his work posted on Instagram under the name *Steelhead_Steve* and at www.facebook.com/steelhead.steve.

Heinz Zöldi of Salzburg, Austria, has been tying flies since he was a boy. His work can be seen on Instagram under the name *noricum_art_flies* and at www.facebook.com/heinz.zoldi.

INDEX

IMAGE CREDITS

Alamy: © Tosh Brown: 134–35; © infocusphotos.com: 196; © Larry Larsen: 133

AP Photo: © Joe Holloway, Jr.: viii

Chris Bain: 33 bottom, 56, 58, 66, 67, 73, 83, 85, 99, 104, 107, 111, 113, 115, 116 bottom

© Chris Bolduc Photography: 39–42

© Bill Buchan: 126, 127, 192 top

Bruce Curtis: ii, x–xiv, 2, 3, 8, 9, 11, 14, 15, 16 bottom, 17, 18, 20–24, 25 center and bottom right, 26, 27 top, 28, 29, 33 top, 34, 35, 37, 38, 44, 45, 47, 53, 54, 55 top, 57, 59, 60 bottom, 61, 62–65, 69, 70–72, 74, 75, 77, 78, 79, 80 bottom, 81, 82, 84, 87, 88, 89 top, 90, 91 bottom, 92–95, 98, 100–103, 105 bottom, 106, 112, 114, 116 top, 117, 118–21, 125, 136–38, 140, 141, 148–51, 153, 154–55, 157, 174, 178, 181, 182, 189 bottom (inset), 192 bottom, 195, 198, 204 top and center, 208 (inset)

Depositphotos: © jannickelson: 187; © lifequestint: 162–63; © sportlibrary: 13; © swisshippo: 204 bottom

Internet Archive: 5, 6, 12, 16 top, 32, 36, 43, 50, 55 bottom, 60 top, 68, 76, 80 top, 86, 7 and 89 bottom, 91 top, 110, 152 bottom

iStock: © Aaltophotography: 180; © ad-foto: 129; © Blue1049: 205; © Bob Balestri: 202; © Coast-to-Coast: 177; © creighton359: 158–59, 164; © digograndi: 156; © Drimafilm: 193 (2); © dt03mbb: 185 top; © dtpearson: 194 top; © FlamingPumpkin: 12; © flownaksala: 128; © g01xm: 132; © GabrielPevide: 194 bottom; © Gooddenka: 184; © Grafissimo: 30, 46, 48, 52, 96, 105, 176 bottom; © JASPERIMAGESCOTLAND: 190; © Jmichl: 170 top; © John_Brueske: 144–45; © johnrandallalves: 172–73; © Diane Labombarbe: 124, 171; © Lindsay_imagery: 175 bottom; © MikeRega: 175 top; © mlharing: 203; © David Gonzalez Rebollo: 167; © Ruskpp: 108; © RyersonClark: 160; © seanfboggs: 142; © shaunl: 161; © snowlizard: 165; © Sportstock: 122–23; © stocknshares: 191; © THEPALMER: 27 bottom; © yykkaa: 183

© Sue Anne King: 143, 146 top and center, 176 top, 186

© Thomas King: 146 bottom

Library of Congress: 4

© Paul McCain: 168, 169, 170 bottom

Courtesy of Sue Post: 19

Shutterstock: © Abstractor (canvas): throughout; © Cat_arch_angel: 139, 152, 179, 188–89, 197, 206–7; © Kozh: 209; © Jiri Kulisek: 130–31; © Fabien Monteil: 166; © nld: 221; © PYRAMIS: 216; © Joseph Sohm: 199, 200–201; © Nikki Montoya Taylor: 147; © Michael Vigliotti: 51; © Yaichatchai (hook): v, 9, 139, 179, 189, 197, 207; © yoyoyai (hook): iii, ix, 1, 11, 19, 29, 31, 49, 97, 109, 123, 125; © Peter Zachar: 185 bottom

U.S. Department of the Interior/U.S. Geological Survey: Map background, throughout

Lee Weil: 25 top left

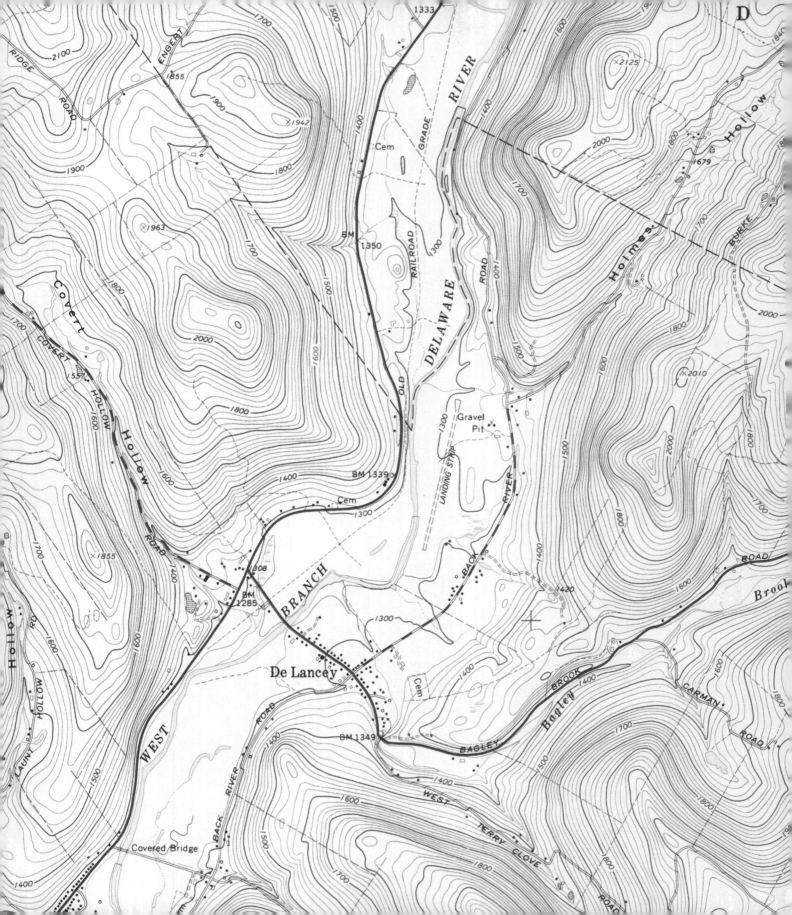